THE SKI MAINTENANCE AND REPAIR HANDBOOK

Seth Masia

Contemporary Books, Inc.
Chicago

Library of Congress Cataloging in Publication Data

Masia, Seth.
    The ski maintenance handbook.

    Includes index.
    1. Skis and skiing—Equipment and supplies—
Maintenance and repairs.   I. Title.
GV854.9.E6M37   1982   796.93028   82-45432
ISBN 0-8092-5737-8   AACR2

Illustrations by Seth Masia

Copyright © 1982 by Seth Masia
Published by Contemporary Books, Inc.
180 North Michigan Avenue, Chicago, Illinois 60601
Manufactured in the United States of America
Library of Congress Catalog Card Number: 82-45432
International Standard Book Number: 0-8092-5737-8

Published simultaneously in Canada by
Beaverbooks, Ltd.
150 Lesmill Road
Don Mills, Ontario M3B 2T5
Canada

Contents

PART IV: POLES AND GOGGLES

Acknowledgments

Some of this material originally appeared in slightly different form in the pages of *SKI Magazine* or in *SKI Business*. I would like to thank the editor of *SKI*, Dick Needham, for permission to use it again.

I can't begin to name all the people within the ski industry who have offered me useful tips or good advice through the years, much of which is incorporated here. A few names stand out: Dick Bohr and the crowd at The Ski Haus; The Stage-coach crew, especially Peter McNair; John Fry at *SKI*; and a whole army of technoids, including Ken Harrell, Bob Rief, John Lovett, John Howe, Sven Coomer, Joe Campisi, Ken Phelps, Bruce Barrows, Hermann Schultes, Peter Weaver, Bob Quinn, John Perryman, John Douglas, Maurice Woehrle, Barry Bryant, Craig Baumann, Bob Mignone, Peter Buser, Dave Calapp, Bill Johnson, Mike Brady, Tim Kohl, David Stewart, Danny Mornet, and on and on. Frank Ledermann did the photo processing and made me look good.

I also learned a hell of a lot from some friends who happen to be very good at breaking equipment, especially Bulldozer Barry and Suitcase. Most of all, I owe thanks to Catherine Williams, who tolerated the clutter, posed for the photos, read the manuscript, and forced me to explain everything clearly. This book is dedicated to her and to good skiers everywhere.

Introduction:
Doing Quality Work

Every sport has its benchmark, the simple skill that separates the dilettantes from the aficionados. Rivermen used to spot a fellow fastwater expert by his J-stroke—if you had a J-stroke, you knew how to handle a canoe, and if you didn't, well, you just didn't. A climber has either led, or he hasn't; top-roping doesn't count. Real drivers know how to double-clutch. Blue-water sailors know their celestial. And so on.

Some skiers may argue that the benchmark for us is posses-sion of a carved turn, or experience in bottomless Utah powder, or an FIS card, or an adventure down Corbett's Couloir, or a Nastar Gold medal. But I always look at a skier's bases.

I can tell a lot about the way skiers turn, and about their attitude toward the sport, by looking at their bases and edges. I can tell whether they spend too much time on their tails, usually carve their turns, ski with legs locked together or with good independent leg action; whether they stem; whether one leg is stronger than the other; whether they swivel-turn in the bumps. Most of all, I can tell from the condition of their skis whether they are interested in improving or they are terminal intermediates.

It may be unfair to say that a good skier—one who skis easily and aggressively in all kinds of terrain—is a terminal case if he doesn't tune his skis regularly. But I've never met a skier whose skills I really respect who doesn't run a thumb over his edges once a day. Nor have I met a really good skier who hasn't figured out a way to make his boots fit really well. If you're going to do high-quality work at anything, you need the right tools. Skis and boots are the skier's tools.

The fact is that you can't ski at the expert level with a marginal boot fit or concave bases or rusty edges, any more than you can drive well with bald tires, loose steering, and gone-for-good shocks. This book will show you how to hone your skiing tools and thereby improve your skiing. But, just as tuning your skis and boots just right is the prerequisite to expert-level skiing, having the right tools and a proper workbench is the prerequisite to tuning skis properly.

Setting Up

You will need a solid workbench that is long enough to hold your skis, and has a ski vise screwed to it. An ordinary steel-jaw, hardware-store vise will certainly damage your bases and edges. Order a proper vise through your local ski shop. Spend enough to buy a good, solid vise, not a lightweight portable racer's vise. Get something that will screw permanently to your bench. Geze, Beconta, U.S. Ski Wax, Toko, Ski Kare, Ski Accessories Company, Kwik, Concepts Design, Alpine Crafts, Fontaine, Reliable Racing Supply, and Hertel distribute this kind of vise. (See Appendix D at the end of this book for addresses.)

You will need a new, sharp file; a 10-inch mill bastard file is best to start with. Also necessary is a wire brush or file cleaner to keep the file in cutting condition. You'll need a high-quality spring-steel scraper, a pocket whetstone or piece of emery paper, an assortment of ski waxes, and a waxing iron. Use an old clothing iron—pick one up at a garage sale for $10. It will be a lot more dependable than the fragile folding travel irons that ski shops sell. Buy inexpensive tool-steel files at a hardware store (about $3 each) or expensive Swedish steel files in a ski shop (about $8 each). The pocket stone can be found at a good hardware store or sporting goods outfit. The scraper and wax are available at all ski shops.

Set up your workbench in a well-lighted, well-ventilated, well-heated area. You can't do good work in the dark, or in a hurry, and a job done in a cold garage is bound to be done quickly and badly.

Finally, ski tuning is a craft. It's very simple and straightforward, but it takes practice. As you get better at it, the job becomes easier and the results improve. Before working on your expensive new skis, practice a few hours on your old skis. The old skis will work better for the time you spend, and you'll be less likely to damage your new skis.

Like any craft, ski tuning is a skill you can take pride in. Working smoothly with good tools is a sensuous thing, and a ski in fine condition is among man's most elegant artifacts. Enjoy the craft and it will help you enjoy the sport more fully.

PART I
SKIS

1

When Skis Are New

When a ski arrives at a ski shop, carefully packaged in a plastic sleeve and a cardboard box, it's not yet ready for the snow. Obviously, it still needs bindings. Less obviously, it still needs a careful tune-up and waxing.

This is true of all skis, even those called "factory tuned," which are shipped with a coat of wax in place. The wax is evidence that the factory is concerned about the chance that the edges will rust during the long sea voyage on a container ship from some European port to the U.S. Customs shed. But all factory tuning jobs are done on high-speed machines, not by hand. And automatic machinery simply doesn't do a very good job of tuning skis.

To understand why this is so you should first know something about the way skis are built. The component parts of a ski—its core, its fiberglass and aluminum structural layers, its steel edges and running surface, its topskin and protective plastic or aluminum top edges, are all coated with strong phenolic or epoxy adhesives and assembled together in a precisely machined steel mold. This mold is then placed in a large hydraulic press,

where the components are cooked at anywhere between 210°
and 300° F., depending on the type of glue, and pressed at about
150 pounds per square inch. The adhesive liquefies and is
pressed into every microscopic gap and pore in the structure.
After 15 or 20 minutes the mold is allowed to cool, it is
removed from the press, and the ski is levered out, still quite
warm.

After the ski returns to room temperature the finishing
operations begin. All the flash and excess resin are ground off,
top and bottom are quickly sanded smooth, and the ski is sent to
the silk-screening room for a bright-colored paint job.

The ski is now cool enough to handle, but it is not yet stable.
The resins inside are still curing, even two days later. If you
have ever worked with fiberglass to repair a boat or auto body,
you know that the fast-cure resins are not the strongest. The
strongest resins cure fairly slowly, so that their molecules can
cross-link thoroughly and completely. The bonds in skis have to
be even stronger than the bonds in civil aircraft, so the epoxies
used are generally of the slower-curing variety. The ski under-
goes minor dimensional changes during this slow-cure period.
Most ski factories can't afford to let skis stack up in a curing
room while this process is completed. The final base grind is
normally done before the ski is silk-screened.

Why New Skis Are Not Flat

The final base grind leaves the edges sharp and square and
the base fairly flat, almost flat enough to ski on. Final dimensional variations as the ski finishes curing will put bulges or
hollows in the base; it's not at all unusual for a new ski to
arrive at the ski shop concave or convex or both.

In addition, the final base grind is done on automatic
equipment—the ski is fed across the grinding wheels by a
moving belt. Theoretically, power-fed operations should be
smoother and more consistent than hand-fed work, but that's
not the way it works out: powerfeed variations arising from
worn belts, out-of-round drive wheels, current fluctuations,

According to the run-out gauge, this brand-new ski, with the manufacturer's label still stuck to the base, is concave by .030—enough to affect
skiability.

and so on frequently produce longitudinal waves in the finished
base.

A fast coat of wax can cover some of these waves and
bulges, but only until the skis touch the snow. If you want to be
assured of skiing on a flat, smooth ski, a ski that runs and turns
the way it was designed to do, it's necessary to hand-tune it
first, filing it flat and ironing a coat of wax deep into the
polyethylene base. Only hand-filling or careful wet-sanding on
a specially designed platen tuning machine can make a ski flat
enough for high-performance skiing.

How Flat Is Flat?

A really flat ski is level across its width within about .002
inch—two one-thousandths of an inch. To measure this minute

dimension would require the precision of a micrometer or a mechanic's run-out gauge. Most good skiers can, however, actually feel the difference between a flat ski and a ski that's concave or convex by .005 inch. Racers can feel the difference at less than .001 inch. I've seen brand-new skis, fresh out of the factory wrapping, that are off by .06 inch or more.

Ski base profiles.

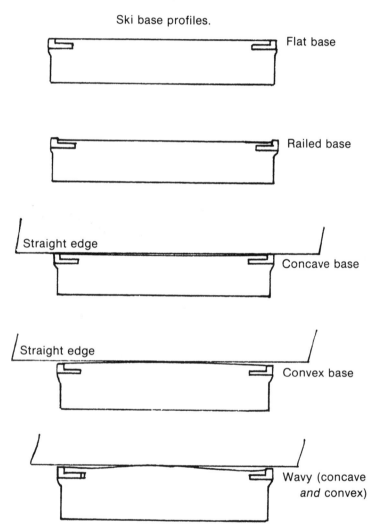

Flat base

Railed base

Straight edge
Concave base

Straight edge
Convex base

Wavy (concave *and* convex)

While you would need sensitive instruments to *measure* this amount of deviation, you *can see* it. Place a ski in a vise, base up, and hang a light source over the ski tip. Any white light bulb, 60 watts or stronger, will do. I use an articulated desk lamp clamped to the end of my workbench, but an ordinary auto shop trouble light works just as well. Place a good straight edge, either a carpenter's steel rule or the clean edge of a steel ski scraper, across the base and sight up into the light. Light should shine through the plastic base in a smooth, even line across the ski. Bright spots and dark spots indicate that the base is wavy.

Concave Bases

If the scraper rests squarely on the two steel edges and light appears under the scraper at the center of the ski sole, the ski is concave. If you try to ski it, it will feel edgy, recalcitrant—it won't want to turn. It will want to run fast, in a straight line, and to turn you'll have to unweight very aggressively—you may actually have to jump and swivel the skis while they're off the snow. Concave skis are exhausting and frustrating—and can even be dangerous. It's easy to catch an uphill edge with concave skis. Half the trouble inexperienced skiers have with their equipment is due to bases that are worn concave.

Prepare a straight edge or sharp scraper by filing one side of a steel scraper into a smooth, even edge.

With the straight edge of the scraper held against the base of the ski, sight into a strong light. This ski is slightly concave, with a high spot just to the left of the center groove. It needs to be filed flat.

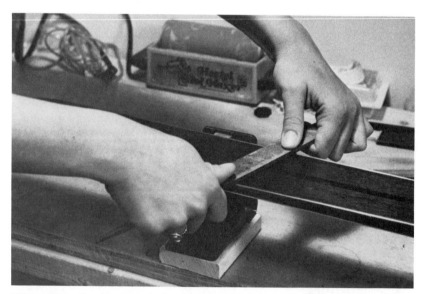

When filing for flatness, hold the file flat against the ski base, with your thumbs placed over the ski edges. The tang of the file should be in the right hand. Push the file in long, even strokes.

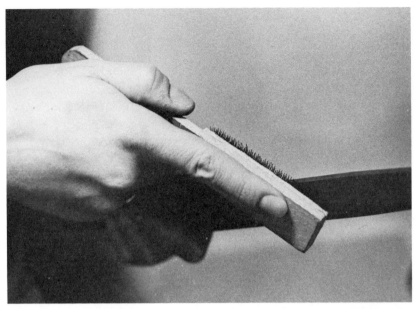

Clean the file frequently with a wire file brush.

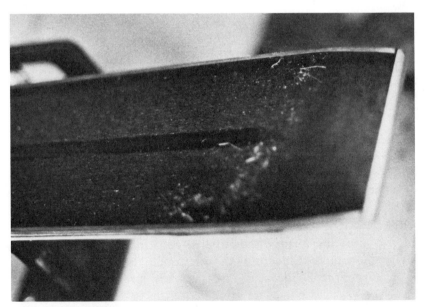

Clean the ski base with a rag to remove these metal filings. Wipe them off after every few file strokes to avoid grinding them into the base.

Flat Filing

Make concave skis flat by filing the steel edges down level with the polyethylene sole. If the concavity is severe, you will need a very aggressive file, like a 12-inch double-cut. Clamp the ski very solidly. Scrape off any wax or adhesive, using your steel scraper. Bend it slightly to get down into the concavity, but don't scrape so hard as to remove any more plastic.

Now you're ready to file. Inspect the edges of your new skis. If they have one-piece, continuous edges, you may file from either end—either tip to tail or tail to tip. If they have cracked edges, made with hairline fissures every inch or so, you can file only tip to tail. You will find cracked edges most often on slalom skis, on some soft mogul skis, and on powder skis.

Since the teeth of most files are oriented at about a 30-degree angle across the width of the file body, to put the teeth at an efficient cutting angle to the ski base the file should be held at about a 45-degree angle to the ski's length. The file will cut in one direction only. If you are going to push the file along, hold the tang in your right hand, the "off" end in your left. Place the file flat on the ski base, with a thumb placed over each edge of the ski on top of the file to place pressure right on the edges. Now push the file along, holding it at that 45-degree angle, and feel it cut. Use moderate pressure—if the file is new and sharp, you can actually see the steel filings curling off the edges. Push the file in long, smooth strokes. If it feels like it's catching and skipping, hold the file at a slightly different angle or alter the pressure—skipping means that you will wind up with a slightly scalloped and very unpredictable edge.

Most important: keep the file and the ski base clean. Every third or fourth stroke, clean the file with your wire brush; turn the file over after every stroke to expose the clean teeth on the other side. Each time you clean the file, run a clean rag or paper towel down the ski to remove the metal shavings. Otherwise the file will drive tiny bits of steel into the soft plastic, creating a slow, sticky, turn-resisting surface.

If you would rather pull the file along the base, follow the same directions but hold the tang in your left hand.

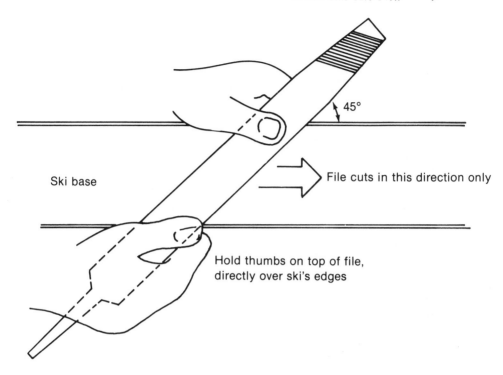

45°

Ski base

File cuts in this direction only

Hold thumbs on top of file,
directly over ski's edges

Convex Bases

If, when you inspect the base with your scraper edge, the
scraper rocks from edge to edge on a fulcrum near the middle
of the sole, then the ski is convex. It will swivel sometimes
when you want it to track. When you're trying to run straight
it will wander right and left and may try to cross over the
other ski's tip. It won't bite very aggressively on hard snow and
will usually feel very unpredictable. You must flatten it by
removing enough plastic to make the sole level with the edges.

You can sometimes do this with a sharp steel scraper. Use a
brand-new scraper or file a clean, straight sharp edge in an old
scraper by clamping it in a vise and filing lengthwise along the
edge. Holding the scraper firmly in both hands, and being
careful not to bend it, scrape the length of the ski. The excess
polyethylene should come off in thin, clean sheets and curls. If
the scraper skips or catches, it isn't sharp enough or you're

holding it at the wrong angle or pressing too hard. Be smooth. You don't want to scrape steps into the base.

Filing the convex base down is easier and smoother than filing a concave base, but you have to stop often to clean the accumulating plastic from the file teeth.

In any filing operation, draw the file only in its cutting direction—don't drag it back along the ski base in the no-cut direction. That only dulls the teeth of the file (they can't be resharpened; a dull file must be replaced) and drives shavings into the plastic base. Check your progress every few minutes by sighting under the straight edge and stop filing when the ski looks flat. No sense in wasting time and elbow grease, not to mention base material.

It's important to check your progress at several points along the ski's length. I've seen skis that were convex at the shovel and tail and concave in the middle. You want to be sure the ski is flat along its full length.

This is the toughest job you will ever have to do on your skis, but a daily or weekly touch-up with the file will prevent them from becoming so concave or convex again. When both skis are flat and smooth, clean your file, take a short rest, and then get ready for a quick edge-filing.

Edge Filing

New skis usually don't need much in the way of edge-filing—the filing operation to flatten the skis usually takes enough metal off to leave a sharp, clean edge. Edges should be sharp enough to shave a thin curl off the flat of a fingernail. A quick once-over will clean up any bad burrs left over from the previous filing. Edge-, or side-filing is tricky: you have to run the file along the edge in the cutting direction (tang trailing), while constantly holding it at a right angle with the flat base. This is most easily done with a file holder designed for the purpose.

File holders are easy to get at most ski shops. Make sure the one you get fits your file. I'm not impressed with most com-

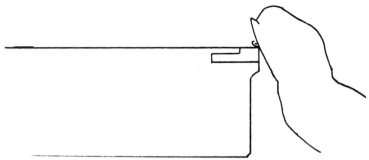

Ski edge is sharp when it will shave a curl off your fingernail

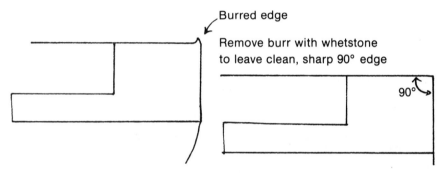

Burred edge

Remove burr with whetstone
to leave clean, sharp 90° edge

90°

mercially available edge files. These are usually small pocket-sized devices meant for use on the hill. The file blades supplied with them are rarely very good—they're either too small, with an inefficient crosshatch tooth pattern, or too aggressive, with big razorlike teeth that take off huge metal shavings with each stroke. Your best bet for edge-filing is an ordinary eight-inch mill bastard file.

If you want to try edge-filing without a file holder—and most experienced tuners don't bother with holders—lock the ski in the vise with the base facing away from you, edge up. Hold the file against the edge with your hand curled over and your knuckles resting on the base, as a guide. File in long, smooth strokes, pressing lightly. Clean the file frequently and brush the shavings off the sidewall and base.

When you finish an edge, take your whetstone or a piece of emery cloth and run it lightly down the full length of the edge once on the side, once flat with the base. This removes the tiny burrs left by the file. A burred edge looks and feels sharp. But it's very easy to catch an edge and fall—burred edges feel a lot like a concave ski.

The last filing operation knocks the sharp edge off the aluminum tip and tail protectors. This is important: in wet snow and on moguls, sharp edges at the ski's extremities, especially at the tail, can hang up and spill you. Clamp the ski with its base up and file all the edges and corners of the tail protector to smooth, round surfaces. Do the same for the tip protector. Think of this as a safety measure.

Clean up all the metal and plastic shavings, plug in your waxing iron, and reach for a bar of base wax.

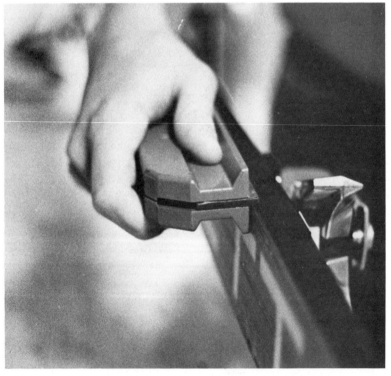

Learn to edge-file using a file holder to get a perfect 90-degree edge.

Later, learn to hold a mill bastard file at the 90-degree angle by curling the knuckles under and resting them against the ski base as a guide. Below, file the tip and tail protectors round, so their sharp edges won't catch in the sides of moguls.

Use your whetstone to remove the burr left by the steel file . . .

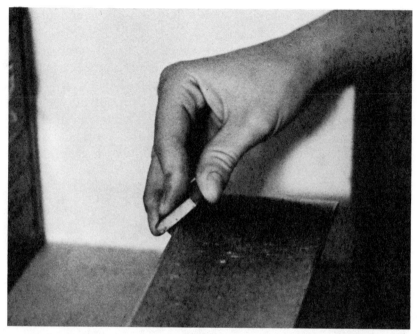

. . . and to dull the tip and tail slightly. Tip and tail dulling is best left to do on the hill.

Waxing

Base wax is the standard wide-spectrum wax available from each manufacturer, the moderate-temperature wax to which hardeners are added in mixing up cold-weather waxes. Look at the wax maker's mixing chart for the proper base wax to use in sealing a new pair of soles. Toko's base wax is red; Holmenkol's wide-spectrum wax is blue; Slik's is red. If you don't have the proper base wax, no matter—any wax is better than no wax, for the same reason that any oil is better than no oil when your car engine is down a quart.

Very simply, wax seals the base and protects it against oxidation. An oxidized base doesn't bead water and is slow and sticky. Polyethylene does oxidize, and ultraviolet radiation speeds the oxidation process greatly. There's a lot of UV light flying around on a bright winter day, especially at high altitudes. It burns your eyes and your nose. It also breaks down the long, tough molecules in polyethylene, so they'll combine with free oxygen from the atmosphere. The only thing between your bases and the oxygen is a good coat of sealer wax. Not to mention that wax glides more smoothly than polyethylene.

Set your iron's thermostat for *wool*. Melt the end of the bar of wax on the sole of the iron, with the iron's tip held against the ski's base. Drip a long bead of wax down the length of the

Hold a bar of wax against the base of your waxing iron and, with the tip of the iron held lightly against the ski base, drip a long bead of wax up one side of the base and back down the other.

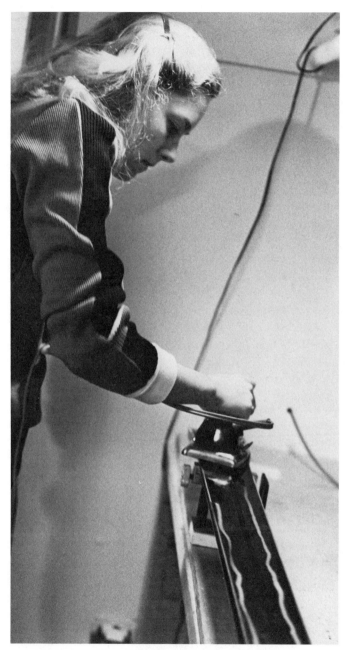

Iron the wax in thoroughly. Keep the iron moving.

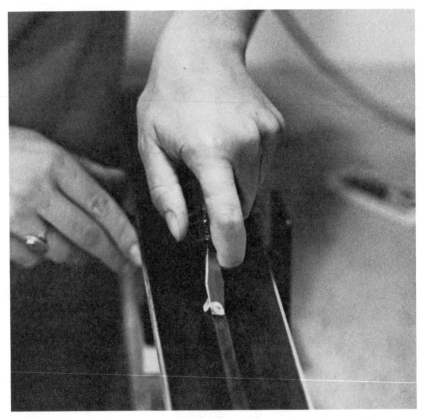

Scrape the wax smooth with a plastic scraper, then clean out the base groove with a dull screwdriver.

ski on one side of the center groove, then up the other side. Set the wax aside and iron the bead into the base thoroughly. Keep the iron moving so you don't burn the wax, but melt it in deep.

Don't worry about damaging the ski—remember that it was molded well above the boiling temperature of water and that melted wax isn't even hot enough to burn your skin much. Many skis—most metal skis, for instance—will bend over backward, acquiring an interesting reverse camber, as their bottom layers expand with the heat. Don't worry about it.

When the wax is thoroughly worked in, let the ski cool until the wax begins to look dry and then take it out of the vise and do the other one. Leave the thick coat of wax in place; it will protect the base and edges in transit.

If you are going to race, the wax should be scraped and buffed to a mirror finish. Otherwise, leave a thick coat to protect the base and edges while the skis are on top of your car.

Clean up your workbench and grab a beer. It's almost guaranteed to snow tonight.

2

Keeping at It

Now that your skis are flat, sharp, and sealed—better than new—you will find that discipline will keep them that way with minimum effort. By discipline I mean the simple determination to find 10 minutes each week in which to touch up your skis. Running the file over your skis lightly after two days of skiing will keep them flat. If, on the other hand, you let your tuning go for weeks at a time, when you finally get around to it you will find your skis very concave again. The soft plastic wears out much faster than hard steel edges.

If you ski each weekend, the best time to tune your skis is immediately upon arriving home. That way you will clean the road grime off your bases and bindings before corrosion sets in. Most skiers I know are exhausted on Sunday night and just like to leave their skis standing in the closet until the following weekend. If your skis travel on top of the car, a ski bag will save you the trouble of cleaning them when you arrive home. Open it when you get home so the skis will dry out thoroughly. Then you can pull the skis out Thursday night, before you pack up the socks and turtlenecks, and get them ready for the first run Saturday morning.

In addition to the tools you have already acquired, you will now need a polyethylene candle, a sharp knife, and a bottle of wax remover. Clamp a ski in the vise, base up, and clean the base and the edges with a rag. Scrape off as much of the old wax as you can, using the steel scraper. Be sure not to bend the scraper; you don't want to remove any plastic. Finish the job with wax remover.

Patching Gouges

Now inspect the base for rock damage. Dings and gouges should be repaired promptly, especially if they are near an edge. Water seeping through a deep gouge near an edge can rust the steel key-slot anchors holding the edge in place. Use the end of a sharp knife to clean any dirt or old wax out of the gouges and cut off any loose flaps or strings of plastic.

Choose one gouge to work on first. Place a sheet of metal— an old cookie tin, for instance, or a cheap aluminum pie plate— under the ski to catch any drippings from the polyethylene candle. The candle will burn with a more subdued, controllable flame if you cut it lengthwise into four thin strips. This is a tough job, even with a very sharp knife. Don't hurt yourself. Now place your steel scraper flat on the ski base to catch drippings alongside the gouge and light the end of the candle with a lighter or a kitchen match.

As the candle begins to burn with a low blue flame, hold it down very close to the gouge you want to fill and let the molten plastic flow into the gouge. Don't let the candle drip— there should be constant contact between the molten candle end and the base material. The candle will flow slowly at first, and the liquid will congeal quickly. Keep turning the candle so it burns evenly and move it along the length of the gouge, flowing the plastic in to fill the ditch. If the gouge runs over the edge of the ski, don't worry—just be sure the cookie tin is there to catch any drippings over the edge. *Don't* allow the molten polyethylene to drip on anything flammable, or on linoleum, or on your shoes or skin. The stuff is like napalm—it burns fiercely. It will go out right away, but, boy, does it hurt.

The flame will soon begin to turn yellow, and plastic will fall off the end of the candle much more quickly. At this point blow the candle out and start over with a cool one. Working with a hot, yellow-burning candle or working with a candle held too high above the ski's base, will lead to carbon deposits flowing into the gouge you are patching. The black flakes in the molten plastic look pretty bad when the stuff hardens. They also weaken the bond between the patch and the base material and probably slow the ski down as well. One of the advantages of slicing your candle into four strips is that, after extinguishing a too-hot strip, you can immediately light a cool one and proceed with the job. Put the old strip on the cookie tin to cool. Rotate your four candle strips until the job is done.

Fill very deep gouges
in layers

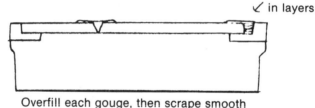

Overfill each gouge, then scrape smooth

Overfill each gouge. The final hardened patch should be higher than the surrounding base material so that you can scrape it down to a level surface.

If you are hesitant about working with an open flame this way, think about buying one of the commercial base-patching tools. They look and work like soldering irons, but have broad spoonlike heated tips for melting and smoothing polyethylene strips. And electrically melted polyethylene won't form carbon deposits. Either way, patching P-tex goes quickly and easily once you've become comfortable with the job.

The plastic patches cool pretty quickly. As soon as they are hard, use your sharpened scraper to flatten them. Then get out your file and do a quick filing job, leaving the base smooth and flat along its entire length. If you ran your ski's edges over any rocks, you will feel the burrs when you do this job. Make sure you file the burrs flat with the base. Unfortunately, there is nothing you can do to fill the gouges in the steel edges.

Daily Filing

Next, edge-file the ski, paying particular attention to reducing rock burrs. Use your pocket stone to finish the edge, just as you did when the skis were brand-new. Then hot-wax. Turn the ski over and check the binding for loose screws and damaged parts (see Chapter 11). Put the skis back in their bag and go pack your duds.

I can't overstress the importance of doing this drill regularly. Pros do it daily. Racers, of course, tune and wax each night. So do good instructors. If you do it daily, it takes no more than 10 minutes. If you do it twice each season, it takes an hour; both you and your edges will be rusty.

The most time-consuming bit in the maintenance drill is the patching. If you do it daily, you will have little or no patching to do each day, except in the late spring. One small ding is a quick, no-fuss repair. Repairing a dozen on each ski, the harvest of weeks of neglect, is a major task.

3

Performance Tuning

Performance tuning is not just for racers. Picking the right wax consistently will, in fact, make skiing easier. It will make your skis glide smoothly through those patches of wet, sticky snow that normally throw you off balance, it will make turns easier to initiate, and it will improve gliding distance on the flats so you won't do as much walking and climbing as your unwaxed friends. Payoff: more skiing, less sweat.

Detuning Skis

There is more to performance tuning than picking the right wax, though. You can actually make a pair of skis behave "stiffer" or "softer" by filing and sharpening them appropriately. A little handiwork with a file can turn a recalcitrant, straight-running missile into an easy-turning pussycat. Long skis are stable in part because they grip well at the ends, where they have the most leverage over your legs. If you reduce the ski's grip at shovel and tail, it will behave like a much shorter, more maneuverable ski. It will swivel more easily on moguls and in

24

heavy or crusted snow. Then, by gradually restoring edge bite at the extremities, you can regain the ski's long-ski performance. This dull 'em and tune 'em process can help an intermediate skier learn to handle a longer ski, or it can be used to detune a hard-snow ski for soft-snow conditions.

There are two ways to detune skis. You can simply dull the edges at tip and tail, or you can file the bottom convex. In either case, make sure the center of the ski is left with a flat sole and sharp, clean edges.

For most eastern and midwestern skiers, the best bet is to dull the edges. Start by rounding off the aluminum tail bar, using a mill bastard file. Round off all corners and edges. Then, using your whetstone or emery cloth, dull the edges for a few inches in from the tail bar and for an equivalent distance back from the contact point (the widest part of the ski) and up into the tip. How far back you dull the edges depends on how "short" you want the skis to behave. A six-inch dull-back is about the limit. You would do best to dull the tip and tail only two inches at first, then go skiing; if the ski still feels long and awkward, use your pocket whetstone to dull the edges an additional two inches, and so on.

It is possible to overdo the edge dulling; in fact, even experienced ski tuners do it all the time on demo skis they lend out in ski shops. I picked up a pair of brand-new Dynastars at a shop in Sun Valley one day, expecting great things. But up at Warm Springs, the skis were just plain bad. A good giant slalom ski should be stable and should cut into the snow smoothly, progressively, and predictably when you roll it up on edge. This ski, fresh off the truck from the factory and carefully hand-tuned, wandered around sideways and, when edged, grabbed and skipped. When I checked the skis with a true bar I found they were flat. The problem was that the tuner had dulled the edges back too far.

This happens a lot. When ski shops send out long skis they don't often believe that the customer really wants a 208 or a 204. So they dull the edges at the tip and tail aggressively to make the ski behave like a 195. With the edges round at the shovel the skis wouldn't bite. They washed out and kicked instead.

That night I ran the skis over a wet-sander in the back of another ski shop and made sure the edges were square and sharp right to the ends. The next morning they behaved just right: smooth, stable, predictable. Great skis.

The lesson is that you can ruin a good pair of skis with unnecessary dulling. Edge-dulling should be done on the hill, using a pocket stone; it should be done only as necessary to make the skis comfortable, and no more.

The other technique for detuning skis is to file the base so it is slightly convex. This process is advocated by a lot of very good soft-snow skiers, including the race-tuning department at the K2 factory and many top western instructors. The convexity is subtle—no more than a hundredth of an inch—but it's enough to keep the skis from hooking and permit a smooth, rolling technique with little sacrifice in edging or carving ability.

The easiest way to file skis convex is to wrap duct tape around one end of your file when you file it to flatten it for the first time. The tape holds the file at a shallow angle to the base as you file. Eight or ten strokes on each edge should be enough to put a hundredth-inch convexity on a new ski base, and the K2 technical people say that should last the life of the ski. I doubt it, unless all you ski in is deep, soft powder, and you always have a fresh coat of wax on the bases.

The key to the dulling business is that sharp ends bite and dull ends slide. Thus you can cure some tricky ski problems. Are your tails so stiff that the ski seems to "rudder" (arrow) straight ahead? Dull the tails only, to balance the ski. Does your ski wash out when you try to initiate a quick, abrupt turn on very hard snow? Oversharpen the shovel, putting an acute angle into the edge instead of the normal 90-degree angle. Fifteen minutes of experimentation each morning will give you the skis you need for the day.

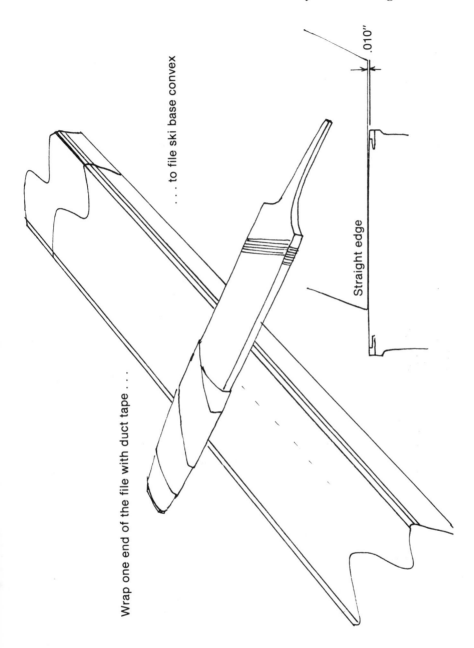

Wrap one end of the file with duct tape . . . . . . to file ski base convex

.010"

Straight edge

Waxing for Speed

Ski wax is a bit like motor oil: always having some wax on the base is better than having no wax, though in the long run you will be better off not to mix brands. As the waxing chart (Appendix C) shows, every wax manufacturer uses a different color-coding system, and some have more than one system. Several wide-spectrum waxes are available, and they are a good bet for the recreational skier. The racer, or the professional skier who wants the best glide in all conditions, should select one brand or system and stick with it, learning it well.

Waxing theory is pretty simple. Snow itself is composed of hard-edged crystals and is quite abrasive. The ski can't glide directly on the sharp points and angles of the snow crystals; it glides instead on a microscopic film of water created as pressure against the snow melts the corners off the crystals, in the same way that pressing an ice cube against the side of a glass melts it to conform to the glass. The ski slides best when this film of water takes the form of tiny individual droplets, which act like ball bearings under the base. If so much snow is melted to form a continuous sheet of water under the base, the suction created by the exclusion of air will slow down the glide. Water is 100 times more viscous than air, so the more air that can be kept in the mix underneath the base, the faster the ski will glide.

Polyethylene is a low-friction material with excellent strength, but it is highly wettable—that is, water sticks to it. If you pour water on an unwaxed ski base, it sheets up instead of beading up into proper ball bearings. Moreover, polyethylene is slightly water-absorbent. It's just porous enough to soak up and retain some moisture. In order to create a smooth, nonwetting, nonabsorptive surface, you must seal the polyethylene with wax.

One of the things that makes polyethylene an ideal ski base material is that it is a close chemical relative of paraffin. Paraffin molecules are very similar in size and composition to the basic ethyl units that link up in astoundingly long chains to

Ski base wettability. From left to right, a freshly waxed ski, a brand-new unwaxed ski, and an old, slightly oxidized, unwaxed ski. A damp sponge has been passed over all three bases. Water beads up and rolls off the fast, waxed base and sheets slightly on the new unwaxed base. The old base wets badly and will glide sluggishly.

make polyethylene, so the paraffin molecules have a good affinity for polyethylene. They fit very neatly into the intermolecular pores in the ski base, and they like to stay there. So paraffin seals the pores well and makes the ski nonabsorptive. Paraffin, a petroleum by-product, is also nonwetting. Water beads up and rolls right off it. So far it looks like an ideal ski wax.

Unfortunately, paraffin is also very soft. This means that the hard, sharp points and edges of snow and ice crystals tend to dig into its soft surface, a process which can prevent a ski from sliding at all. In order to harden the paraffin, wax manufacturers add various "plasticizers," or hardeners, most of them chemical intermediaries between the paraffin and polyethylene molecules. The more plasticizers, the harder the wax. But the more plasticizers, the more wettable the material.

Now very warm snow is high in water content, with big, soft, rounded crystals. Since the edges of the crystals aren't too

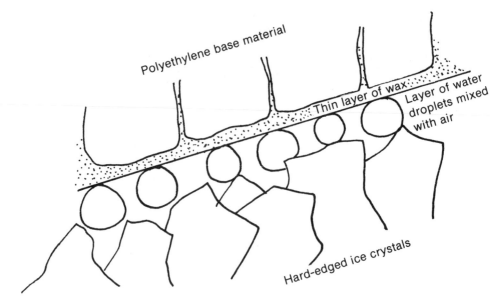

Gliding mechanics

sharp, you can use a fairly soft wax, and since the snow is very wet, you need a nonwetting wax. So "warm" waxes, those formulated for warm and wet snow, are largely paraffin, with a relatively small plasticizer content. Very cold fresh snow contains little moisture and has very small, hard, sharply pointed crystals. You need a much harder wax and can live with a more wettable surface since the snow is largely air anyway. So "cold" waxes are heavy with plasticizers and somewhat further along the continuum toward polyethylene. Your job on any given morning is to judge the water content of the snow and the sharpness of the snow crystals and select a wax with just the right level of hardness and wettability.

The wax manufacturers make that easy by publishing very detailed waxing tables. Study the table that comes with your wax assortment and follow the directions carefully. If you're worried about misjudging the wax, you're better off choosing a slightly harder wax than picking one that is slightly too soft. We have all seen those bitterly cold days when a soft red wax wouldn't slide, when the snow sounds squeaky underfoot because it's so dry, and when the hard crystals, digging into the wax, actually adhere solidly to the ski so they need to be scraped off. A wax that is too hard will work a lot better than one that is too soft.

Come spring, when the snow is wet and slushy, or corned up, a good tactic is to use a reasonably hard base wax—usually red—and carry a bar of softer wax in a small plastic bag, along with your pocket stone. If too much wettability is making your skis sluggish, crayon the warm wax over the hard wax and leave it fairly rough. You can mark a series of Xs the length of the ski, and it will break up the surface tension. It's easy to apply a soft wax over a hard one and impossible to apply a hard wax over a soft one. So wax a bit on the hard side.

Ski waxes generally melt between about 120° and 170° F. The harder the wax, the higher the melting temperature. The hard waxes should be ironed in thoroughly and scraped and polished smooth. In the spring, with the snow very wet, it's often a good idea to apply a thick coat of soft wax by painting it on. Melt a bar of wax in a small saucepan over a low flame. Don't overdo it or the wax will burn. Use a natural-bristle paintbrush just wider than the ski base—a nylon-bristle brush may actually melt in the hot wax. Paint the wax on in long strokes, starting at the tail and moving forward. The "step" formed at the beginning of each stroke will help break up surface tension. Clean out the base groove, too. By introducing an air channel, you may reduce suction in very wet snow.

Waxes may be blended to handle intermediate temperatures. In fact, all wax manufacturers recommend blending. Blending waxes is easy when you are ironing wax in. If the chart calls for, say, one part red and two parts blue, just hold one bar of red wax in a sandwich between two bars of blue wax and press the end of the sandwich against the iron to drip the resulting wax on the ski base. Then iron the mixture in as usual.

Racers can achieve a faster glide by rubbing the first coat of wax into the base with a copper-bristle brush, which helps open pores in the plastic base. One of the wax companies,

Swix, also publishes detailed instructions on hand-sanding the base for faster glide.

If you don't intend to race, some of the newer broad-spectrum waxes can save you the trouble of carefully picking and blending a wax for the day. Some of these formulas are technically very interesting. For instance, Hertel's Hot Sauce is a relatively hard wax, suitable for colder snow. To keep it from wetting out in warm snow, the manufacturer adds an *encapsulated* antiwetting agent; as the wax wears down in the course of the day's skiing, the antiwetting chemical is gradually released to help water bead up for good glide.

Other nonwax-base preparations include a variety of spray-on and wipe-on Teflon substances. These do a pretty good job of beading water, but they are incompatible with wax, and some of them wear off pretty quickly. If you're going to use Maxiglide or one of the other Teflon formulas, start with a wax-free ski base.

A final note of warning: You can rub on all waxes designed for ironing in. However, a few waxes are designed specifically for rubbing, and these waxes should not be ironed. Ironing them will produce a sticky, gummy kind of goop that will have to be scraped down almost to bare plastic to glide at all.

4

Heavy Damage

While skis are very robust, they are also subject to appalling impacts. The most common cause of heavy damage, however, is not dragging skis across rocks, but simple negligence.

Negligence leads to two conditions that will make good skis useless: railing and rust. Skis become railed when you fail to file them flat for any length of time. The plastic sole wears down, leaving the steel edges standing above the surface like the rails that freight trains run on. And a railed ski handles pretty much like a freight train. Cure railing with the biggest, meanest file you can find, plus several hours of hard work, or take the skis to a good ski shop equipped with a wet-belt sander.

Rusted edges result when skis are put away still carrying a thin film of road grime. In addition to diesel oil, microscopic bits of asphalt, sulphur dioxide, and various unburned hydrocarbons, road grime includes a generous helping of road salt and other corrosive chemicals spread by highway departments in an effort to save the lives and property of city folk with bald tires. If you want to know what this stuff does to ski edges, just walk out to the garage and take a look at your car's rocker panels. The first thing to do when you take your skis off the top of your car is to wipe them down with a sponge rinsed in clean, fresh water. Wipe the bindings, too. Then store your skis in some dry place, preferably a heated spot, so they dry out properly.

Once ski edges are badly rusted, the only solution is a long session with the wet-belt sander, which may take off enough material to significantly shorten the life of the ski.

Deep Gouges

A number of different types of damage can be done by impact, most frequently by skiing over rocks. The most common type is a very deep gouge, which sometimes goes right down to the fiberglass or the aluminum backing up the plastic base. Occasionally a flap of plastic is torn free from the underlying material. The repair is tricky, because polyethylene doesn't stick readily to anything but itself. The original base material actually has to be flame-treated on the bonding side in order to glue it permanently to the structural layers.

The best way to repair such a tear is to cut away the damaged sole and thoroughly clean the underlying material. Use emery cloth to clean and roughen the surface and clean it with a strong detergent or some agent that won't damage the surrounding plastic or its bond. Flush the area thoroughly and dry it thoroughly—a hair dryer will help. Then, using a high-quality epoxy, carefully laminate in a sheet of polyethylene base material cut to fit the excised portion exactly. Most good ski shops are prepared to do this patch job. If you are not, you can make a semipermanent patch by dripping in several layers of P-tex candle, building the layers up gradually and allowing them to harden between applications.

Before laying down a new melt, roughen the last melt surface with emery paper and clean it carefully. Sometimes a patch applied this way will be permanent; sometimes it will pop out after a couple of runs.

Use a sharp knife to clean dirt, old wax, and loose plastic out of deep gouges in the base.

The polyethylene candle burns cooler and more evenly if you first slice it lengthwise into quarters.

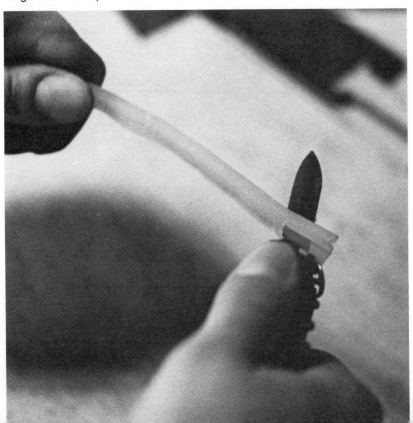

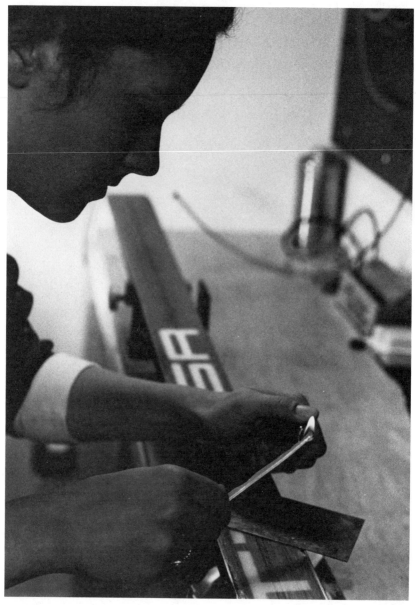

Place a scraper across the ski base to catch the first drippings from the candle and light the end.

Above, flow the molten plastic into the gouge, holding the burning end of the candle right down on the ski base. If the plastic drips in instead of flowing, it will absorb more oxygen, carbonize, and make a weaker patch. Below, overfill the gouge and let it cool between layers if you need more than one application to fill it.

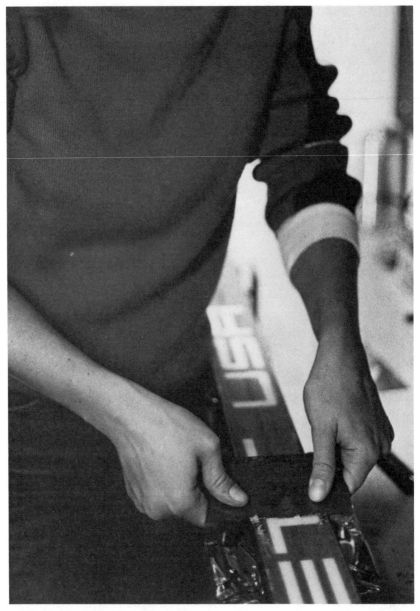

When the patch has set solidly, use a sharp scraper to plane it down flat with the base. Then file flat.

Edge Repairs

The problem is made tougher if the gouge that tore back the flap of base also pulled out a segment of edge. Only a good ski shop will be equipped to remove the damaged edge section and install a new, matching piece. If the edge has merely delaminated at the tip or tail, however, and curled up off one end, you can fix it at home.

Use a sharp knife to dig out any dirt left between the plastic base and the ski's sidewall, then clean the exposed parts of the edge thoroughly with emery cloth. Pry the base back gently and clean up the exposed bonding surfaces with a sharp point; try to scrape out any old glue left in the joint. Then fill the split with epoxy, push the edge back into place, and clamp it tightly after wrapping the repair in wax paper to keep the epoxy from bonding the clamp permanently to the ski. After the repair

This detached edge has delaminated from the ski base and internal structure. Note the pattern of lighter-colored plastic under the clear base, where the edge has pulled out. Clean up the mating surfaces and epoxy the edge back in place.

cures, clean up the epoxy overflow with a file. Then file to flatten and edge-file the ski to make sure the repaired section is uniform with the rest of the running surface.

A few skis with soft or brittle cores can be dented. For instance, older Hexcel and some Hart honeycomb skis can show a dented base because impact with a rock has bent the walls of the honeycomb structure under the impact point. You can't straighten out the core again, but you can fill the depression in the base. Roughen the plastic with emery paper and melt the polyethylene candle into the dent in layers, just the way you'd fill a deep gouge.

On a few skis it's possible to knock the aluminum tail protector out. It's a simple enough matter to clean the mating surfaces and epoxy the tailpiece back in, but it must be done promptly. You don't want a deep notch exposed in the tail, which may, through capillary action, draw water into the core, leading to dry rot and a broken ski. If you have lost the aluminum tail bar, seal the open slot with a good epoxy. Use masking tape to build a dam around the slot and pour the mixed epoxy in until it fills.

Terminal Cases

A ruptured sidewall usually means serious structural damage has been done to the load-carrying layers of the ski. Check carefully for bends, warps, or tiny cracks in the edges, base, and topskin and for delaminations above and below the site of the sidewall break. If you are convinced that the underlying fiberglass or metal layers are still in one strong piece, then you simply must seal the impact-damaged sidewall to prevent water seepage. You can do this with epoxy, wax paper, and a clamp. If the ski's structural layers are damaged, or its core needs repair, the ski will almost certainly break the next time you start cranking turns. Clean it up and hang it over the mantle.

This brings us to the various reasons to retire a ski. Fatigue damage is something you can't do much about. The most common form is a bent ski. Sooner or later you will have a metal-sandwich ski with its tip pointing upward at rather an odd angle. It's actually possible to ski on a bent ski for several days and not notice anything wrong other than a worse-than-usual lack of coordination. It pays, from time to time, to put both skis of a pair down together on a flat surface just to see if the camber and angle of the tip still looks the same on each. Sometimes this is the only way to spot a slightly bent shovel.

If you ski mostly in powder, you can bend a metal-sandwich ski roughly back into shape and finish out the season on it. Bending the ski will help restore its turning characteristics, but the ski will be permanently weakened at the bend site and will inevitably bend again. Bending problems are most serious for bigger guys skiing on shorter metal skis. If you weigh more

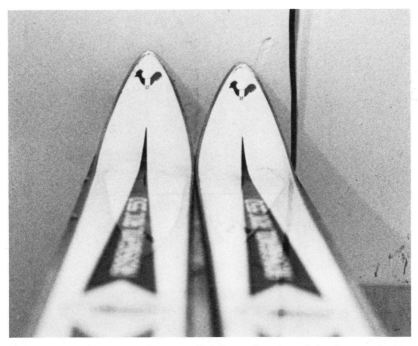

The left ski of this pair is bent slightly at the shovel. It shows up as a slightly higher tip turn-up when the skis are placed together on a flat surface. This pair is still skiable in soft snow but is useless for racing and will probably bend further in time.

than 170 pounds, you will eventually bend any metal giant slalom ski shorter than about 200 cm. Powder skis are whippier and won't deform as easily.

Metal skis also delaminate. Sometimes delamination will show up as a bubble under the edge, usually at the front of the shovel where impacts occur each time you put the edge into a mogul or water bar. Small bubbles can be glued and clamped, but they reappear almost instantly. Major delaminations can be glued back together, but the result is usually an impossibly stiff ski. These failures, and spiral warping, are good reasons to hang 'em up.

After many years of use, skis simply wear out. A friend on the Snowmass ski patrol had a favorite pair of Stratos he had raced on in college and patrolled on for years. He tuned them and patched them religiously, so the base and edges looked nearly new while the top edges were worn down to bare ash. Finally the tiny screws that held the edges in place began showing through the plastic base. Overnight, it seemed, the Stratos disintegrated. The edges fell out. The base fell off. Good-bye, Old Paint.

If the edges are still solid, it is possible to replace the plastic sole. For about $50, a major ski service center can rout out the old base and glue in a brand-new P-tex running surface. It's a good way to get another couple of years' service from a favorite pair of boards. Ask a good local shop where they send this kind of work. Have it done over the summer, since it involves shipping skis long distances.

Ski Shop Damage

It's not supposed to happen, but it does: sometimes a ski shop will damage a pair of skis while mounting the bindings. The shop should be responsible for repairing this kind of damage. It usually involves delaminating the topskin, in which case the ski must be replaced, or pushing out the top edge, which can sometimes be repaired.

On thinner skis, particularly skis for kids, a shop will sometimes mount bindings with adult-size screws, which then either punch right through the base or create a pattern of pimples pushing out the base. Inspect any new children's ski for these pimples. They make the ski impossible to learn on. If you discover this condition long after the fact, simply remove the binding screws, grind the sharp ends off them, put a drop of epoxy into each screw hole, and reinstall the shortened screws. Then file the ski for flatness to level out the bumps.

Topskin damage is more or less unavoidable, and since it's a purely cosmetic problem—minor nicks and scratches—don't worry about it. Aluminum top edges should be inspected frequently for gouges, because they sometimes grow sharp, evil metal splinters, which can cut a hand pretty badly. File these curls of metal down smooth.

Keep an eye on the top edges of skis, especially at the shovel and tail. If the core shows through, immediately patch the worn spot with epoxy to prevent water seepage. Cracks and crazing of the topskin are unimportant, unless the fiberglass under the topskin begins to chip and peel. If the ski is still under warranty, and a deep crack appears in the topskin, by all means return it for service. If it is no longer under warranty, just patch it back together with epoxy and duct tape and keep skiing.

Most good skiers don't worry much about the way the topskins look. It's the people who constantly cross their tips who bang their tops up badly. You can save some embarrassment and a lot of wear and tear by installing a set of Parablacks or other anticrossing devices (ACDs). Some of these machines are pretty flimsy. In general, it's a good idea to avoid the fancier mechanical versions and stick with a simple, tough, one-piece design. Choose one you can remove for airline transport, or it's sure to be knocked off. ACDs serve only one useful purpose: they help keep your tips from crossing. They do not materially affect the ski's damping or stability or even affect its drag in deep snow. One racer I know claims they help him go faster on downhills, though. "If I can't look through my Parablacks, I know my tuck isn't low enough," he says.

5

Storing and Transporting Skis

A fresh tune-up represents a certain amount of work. Don't risk ruining it by mistreating your skis in transit. Be sure the skis are tied together securely, with no chance of scissoring, which ruins the sharpness of the edges. This means that the skis should be locked together with the ski brakes or safety straps, but also secured with a ski tie at the shovel. To protect the polished wax, the racer will cushion the bases with a sheet of newspaper or by using a Racer-Spacer or similar protective ski tie.

Car Travel

It's important to protect skis from road salt. When possible, travel with the skis inside the car, properly bagged to protect the occupants. If the skis can't be wedged securely between the seats, tie them down, perhaps with the rear-seat safety belts, so they won't shift when you corner or brake. If they must go on an external ski rack, be sure they are bagged, even if that merely involves wrapping them with dry-cleaner bags or trash can liners. In fact, plastic bags have the wonderful advantage over expensive nylon ski bags that you can simply toss them out when you arrive at the resort, instead of having to hang a filthy, soaking bag in the bathroom to drip.

Going by Air

Airlines require that skis be bagged. Take extra care with skis shipped by air. Use a good, tough bag and tape the skis together with duct or strapping tape. Ski ties can break or snap loose with the kind of rough handling they get in busy airports, and they are likely to scissor. Remove any attachment that is likely to break off—Parablacks and other anticrossing devices are prime candidates.

I usually travel with several pairs of skis. They all go in a single voluminous nylon bag that cinches tightly at either end to keep the skis bound securely together. When I arrive I can slide the bag into a hatchback rental car or, if the car is too small (which is sometimes the case when I have an additional passenger or two), I can tie the bag, unopened, on top of the ski rack, using a pair of good-quality bungee cords. The bag is unique and hard to lose. Perhaps because it says "SKI" on the outside, it has not yet been sent to Honolulu.

Packing Tools

Pack your file and scraper in your check-through luggage. A 10-inch mill bastard file looks pretty strange in a carry-on bag, and unless you are prepared to spend half an hour explaining to the security police why they shouldn't consider it a weapon, it's better off in the cargo hold. Don't pack it with your skis unless it's in a leather holster, or you may arrive with a strange set of notches worn in the skis.

Some Storage Tips

Skis should be stored in a dry, heated room—not in an

ovenlike attic or a damp basement. File and wax skis before storing them for more than a couple of weeks. The wax will prevent rusting. Tie them to prevent scissoring and stand them in a closet, secured so they can't fall over. This is merely a safety precaution. A pair of falling skis can be lethal. A single pair, or two pair, can be secured simply by putting a screw eye in the wall at shovel height and passing a cord around the skis and through the eye. A family recreation room is a good place to build a ski rack to hold everybody's gear off the floor, out of the way, where it will stay dry and clean.

An advantage of the rec-room ski rack is that when skis are easily visible and accessible they are likely to be tuned more often—it's a good rainy-day endeavor. If skis are buried in a closet, behind the coats and boots, they will be forgotten. You'll drag them out in a hurry while packing for the weekend and discover that the bases are unpatched and unwaxed and that the edges are rusting.

PART II
BOOTS

6

Boot Fit

The most important consideration in buying ski equipment is not ski length or binding adjustment. It's boot fit. If your boots don't fit correctly, nothing else will work properly. Certainly not your skis, for all control of the skis has to pass through the boots, and if your boots are too large, you lose some of the control you should have.

Ironically, while boots have improved vastly in materials, in design, and even in last shape, today's skier is probably skiing in a boot about one size too large. According to Bob Rief, who was product manager for Nordica before being kicked upstairs to a vice-presidency, more than half the skiers buying boots in the United States are sized wrong. One problem is that each European manufacturer has a different idea of what an American size nine should be; another problem is that most people simply don't know what a properly fitted ski boot feels like. They try on two or three boots and buy the most comfortable, or the one that seems to offer the right flex rate. Rief suggests that, for Nordica boots, *racers* go down 1½ to two whole shoe sizes; recreational skiers go down a full size. If you wear a size nine street shoe, you should ski in a size eight Nordica or smaller. Other ski boot companies, of course, have other ideas. Your best bet is to try on lots of boots.

Most ski shops will carry at least two brands of boots: one offering a fairly narrow fit and one offering a wider fit. Some shops carry as many as half a dozen brands. Shop early in the season to take advantage of a full size range. As you try on boots, remember that most boots will stiffen in the cold, and most boots will also stiffen when locked into a binding, which reinforces the thin plastic sole. If the boot that fits best seems a bit too stiff, however, don't worry about it—boot flex can usually be softened dramatically.

A skier's best friend is an experienced boot fitter. Try to deal with a shop you trust, perhaps one that offers a guaranteed fit. However, boots never seem to fit the same way after the first day on the hill. That wonderful, snug, comfortable fit inevitably degenerates into hotspots, shin bruises, cold toes, or heel blisters after a couple of wild runs. And if you spend your first weekend in new boots a six-hour drive from your friendly, local ski shop, you have become, ipso facto, an instant Saturday Night boot fitter. Here's what you need to know.

How Boots Should Fit

Boots should fit snugly but not uncomfortably. Toes should wiggle, but the heel, instep, and ball of the foot should be effectively immobilized. There should be no pressure points over the instep, around the ankle, or against the shin.

Hotspots and pressure points along the sides of the feet, usually at the ball of the foot or along the outside of the metatarsal, can mean the boot is too narrow. The easiest solution is to remove some of the foam from the inner boot at the location of the painful spot. Boots with injection-molded foam inners are easiest to work on. Just slice the foam off in thin layers until the fit is right.

With inners of sewn construction, make a door-shaped incision in the outer lining (usually made of vinyl-coated fabric or nylon fabric) and dig out the foam with a knife point or the end of a spoon. Be careful not to puncture the boot's flow pockets, which are usually located around the heel and ankle. Close the incision with duct tape when the pressure point has been relieved.

Experiencing pain or cramps over the instep, often accompanied by cold toes, means there is too much pressure over the instep. Relieve it by lowering the footbed. First try removing the insole inside the inner boot. If you still need more room, pull out the plastic footbed from under the inner boot and shave it thinner.

A blister on your heel normally means the boot is too wide to immobilize your heel, which rubs the skin raw as it moves around inside the boot. Add a cork heel wedge or a custom-molded orthotic insole (see Chapter 7) to lift the heel into the narrower part of the boot's heel pocket or tape padding on either side of the inner boot for a narrower fit. The latter solution is the better idea if you have a high instep to begin with, since adding a heel wedge can often make a boot tight over the instep. If you do add extra padding around the heel pocket, make sure it fits below the ankle or you will create pressure points over the bony projections of the ankle.

Cold toes, with no additional pain or cramps, may mean the boot is too narrow around the Achilles tendon area, just behind the ankle knobs. There are a couple of important veins here, and constricting them shuts off the flow of warm blood to the toes. Using a sharp knife, carefully remove foam from the Achilles tendon area, working in vertical slices on either side of the tendon.

Most good ski shops carry a variety of boot-fitting aids, including sheets of pressure-sensitive foam padding you can cut to shape to make specific parts of the boot narrower. Remember that you can't relieve a pressure point by adding padding—that only makes the pressure more severe. Relieve pressure by *removing* material.

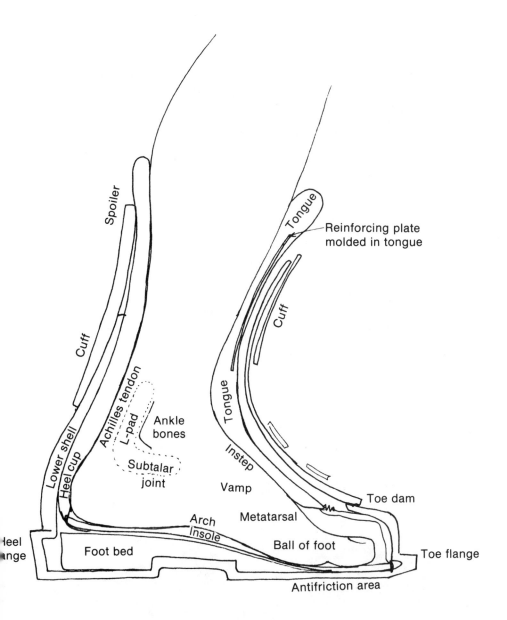

Parts of the boot and foot

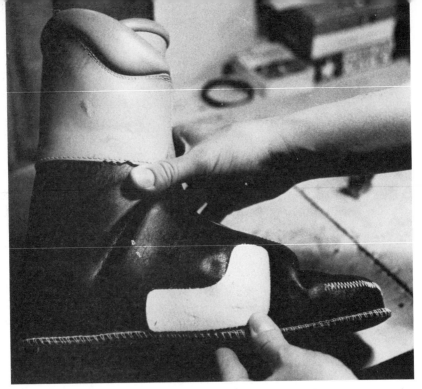

If boots are too wide, add pressure-sensitive adhesive foam sheets to the outside of the inner boot. Here the padding has been placed to narrow the fit in the vamp and forward of the instep. Another common area for adjustment is around the heel.

This boot was too tight around the ankle bones and Achilles tendon, creating a painful hotspot above the heel and cutting off circulation to the toes. The solution was to cut off foam to reduce the pressure.

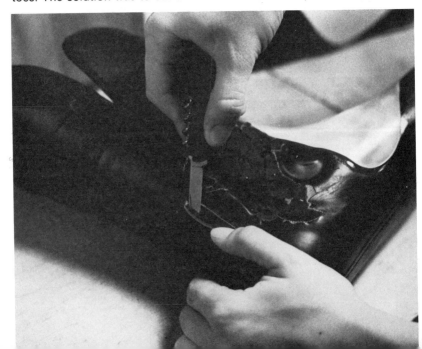

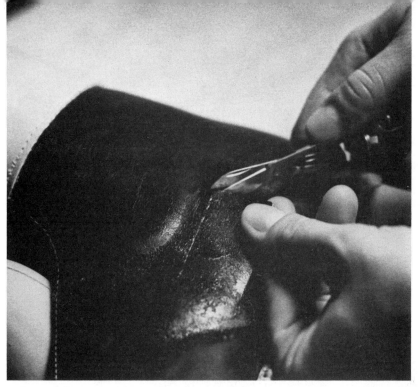

Most boots use sewn-up inners. In order to remove foam padding, it's necessary to cut through the outer fabric of the inner boot. Cut carefully to avoid puncturing flow pockets that may be built into the boot. The flow pocket is a plastic or fabric envelope placed over the foam padding. This pocket is not glued to the outer skin of the inner boot, so you can safely cut around it.

Repairing the Tongue

Tongue problems are tough. There is very little you can do to make an ill-fitting tongue work better, and a tongue that is just a little bit off can do terrible things to tender shins. If your shins hurt, check the following:

- Are your socks or long johns bunched up in front of the shin? Use longer socks and pull them up tight. Also make sure your long johns don't end inside the boot.
- Is the ABS reinforcing plate inside the tongue broken or separated from its foam backing? If so, the tongue should be replaced.

- Is the edge of the tongue curled under itself, or is it deformed from having been stored with the boot closed improperly? Try steaming it back into shape.
- Does the tongue bend over a fulcrum created by the shell top when you flex the boot forward? Try softening the shell or reinforce the back of the tongue with a sheet of fiberglass or plastic.
- Some tongues simply rub the shin raw. Tape a plastic bag around the tongue to make a low-friction surface on the inside.

A few products are designed to reinforce a broken-down tongue. Typically, they consist of a piece of thermosetting plastic that can be molded between your shin and the boot tongue, then baked hard to form a protective, form-fitting shell. Ask a good local boot fitter for help with this stuff, because it can be tricky. It's possible, for example, to mold it in such a way that the untrimmed edge itself becomes a pressure point or interferes with boot flex.

A good shop can also help solve really extreme fit problems by modifying the boot shell. This involves softening the plastic with a hot-air gun or hot-water bath and widening or lengthening the shell, as needed, with a special hydraulic press. Some shops can even weld whole new sections into boots, using a special hot-air welding machine.

7

Making Boots Ski Better

Once the major fitting problems are solved, a boot should ski well. If it is still too stiff to absorb terrain comfortably, or too soft for precise control, the problem can be rectified by modifying the shell.

One of the great things about plastic ski boots is that they are easy to alter. Using an electric drill with a good assortment of bits and grinding wheels, a pop riveter, and some imagination, you can turn the stiffest, hairiest racing boot into a comfortable cruiser or bring a slipper-fit mushbucket up to snuff.

Softening Boot Flex

You can soften any traditional overlap-style boot first by drilling out the locking rivets, then by cutting flex channels in the lower shell. Many boots have flex channels molded in place; all you have to do is cut along the dotted line with a sharp knife—after removing the inner boot, of course. If the boot is of the side-hinge variety, it probably won't have designed-in flex channels. For instance, a popular boot for softening is one of the Lange XL-series racing boots—the XL-1000, XL-R, XL-950, and so on. After drilling out the locking rivets, it's necessary to cut a flex channel down the spine of the lower shell. Do so with a grinding wheel.

Finish off any softening modification by grinding a thinner edge into the bottom of the boot cuff, all the way from the hinge around to the ends of the buckle straps. You can also spray this area with a good Teflon coating. Both tactics will help the cuff slide more freely over the lower shell.

Most Italian-made boots nowadays are built with an external tongue to control flex. Soften flex by grinding lateral flex channels into the external tongue or by grinding its edges thinner. Lubricate the tongue with a Teflon coating wherever buckle straps cross it.

Rear-entry boots—Hansons and Salomons, for instance—present special problems. They offer a limited amount of flex adjustment, but the softest setting may be too firm for some skiers. Soften Hansons by grinding down the stiffening rib on the front of the boot. Grind it a little at a time until the boot feels right and be sure not to weaken the material around the rivets or screws that hold the shell halves together. Salomon boots close with a band that wraps around the cuff. The boots can be softened by cutting or drilling small notches in this band to allow it to stretch more easily.

Stiffening Boot Flex

Most boots can be stiffened by adding locking rivets through the upper cuff and lower shell. A pop riveter will do this job neatly and quickly, or you can ask a ski shop to do it for you. If you would like to experiment before installing permanent rivets, drill the appropriate holes and install machine screws, held in place on the inside of the shell with tee nuts.

A few boots can be stiffened only by adding aluminum strips to the outside of the shell. This process can create more problems than it solves, but it's worth trying before spending $200 for new boots. Aluminum bar stock in all sizes is carried in

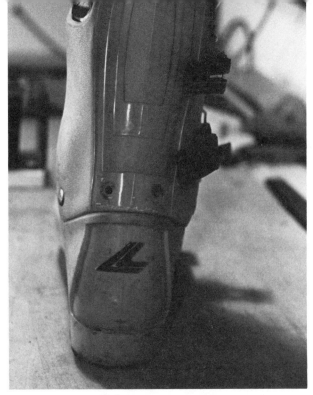

Soften overlap-construction boots by drilling out the locking rivets and cutting or grinding a new flex channel down the back of the lower shell, inside the cuff.

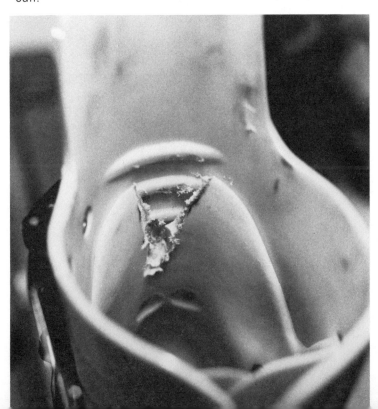

Soften boots with wraparound (rear-hinge) construction by cutting out flex channels down the side of the lower shell, under the cuff.

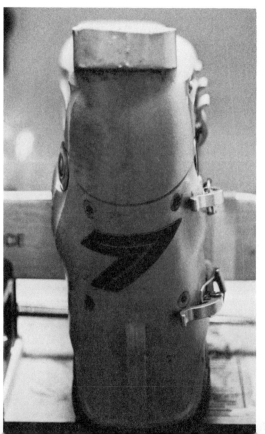

This boot was softened in flex (note missing locking rivets) and the sole was ground for improved canting. Note that the tops of the toe and heel flanges were ground parallel to the sole for correct binding function and that hard use in parking lots has begun to wear down the heel on one side.

most hardware stores. It is easily cut to length and drilled for rivets. When marking boot shells for aluminum stays, be sure the stay won't interfere with buckle closure or binding operation. One stay up the spine should stiffen any boot sufficiently. Secure the lower end solidly so it won't lever its rivet out. Any time you install rivets in polyurethane, use backing washers.

Increasing Forward Lean, Edge Control

You can increase the forward lean of any boot by installing a pad on the back of the inner boot. Make the pad of foam sheet or multiple layers of duct tape.

The most subtle and most important way to improve the way a boot skis is to install a custom-molded footbed. By filling all the voids under the foot, a molded footbed provides greatly improved stability for the foot and faster response: every slight pressure is instantly translated into a movement of the ski, rather than being filtered first through a slight pronation of the foot within the shell.

Expert boot fitters are equipped to make such custom footbeds, and they can be tailored to fit most boots. They will improve anyone's skiing, but they can be expensive—usually $50 to $75. An inexpensive alternative is to mold your own footbed.

Cut two pieces of clean muslin to the shape of the insole of your ski boot. Place one piece on a thick sheet of flexible plastic—a garbage bag will do nicely. Cover this sheet of fabric with a layer of silicone caulk—the kind that comes in caulk-gun tubes, not the thin, runny stuff sold in toothpaste squeeze tubes. The layer should be fairly thin at the toes and ball of the foot, thicker under the arch and around the edges of the heel.

Place the other piece of muslin on top of the caulk and pull up a chair. Take off your sock and, while seated, with no weight on your bare foot, press your foot gently into the soft footbed so it takes an impression of the sole of your foot. Wash any caulk off your foot and repeat the procedure for the other foot, using the other boot's footbed as a pattern. Let the molds cure overnight, cut them away from the garbage bag, slip them into your boots in place of the original insoles, and go skiing.

If the footbeds don't feel quite right, it's easy to make a new pair, pressing your feet down in a slightly altered position. It's dirty, but it's quick and cheap, and you can experiment until you get it right.

Canting

About 10 years ago ski coaches and ski shops began making a lot of noise about canting, or wedging. It was pointed out that because boots of the era made no allowance for the natural outward curve of the leg, most skiers naturally tended to stand on the outside edges of their skis. This meant the skis felt unstable, since they would tend to wander apart in straight running. And it meant the skier had to exaggerate greatly the edging motion to drive the inside edge of the ski into the snow to start a turn.

A ski shop could remedy this situation simply by installing wedges or cants under the skier's bindings, to put the ski flat on the snow when the skier assumed a natural, relaxed stance. At the same time, boot makers began building boots with a designed-in cant. This cant could be as small as half a degree or as large as five degrees; and it was not unusual to find skiers who were overcanted in their new boots so that they tended to stand naturally on their inside edges. Standing thus, they had no difficulty beginning turns; the trouble came in trying to end turns. And they crossed their tips a lot. Again, the solution was to install cants under the bindings, this time with the thick side of the cant over the outside edges of the skis to compensate for overcanting the boots.

Most good skiers with relatively normal legs, skiing in boots of normal height, can adjust automatically for a couple of degrees of cant, and such an adjustment is necessary every time you change boots. If your new boots differ by two degrees or more of cant from your old boots, you may find skiing awkward until you compensate for the change by installing wedges.

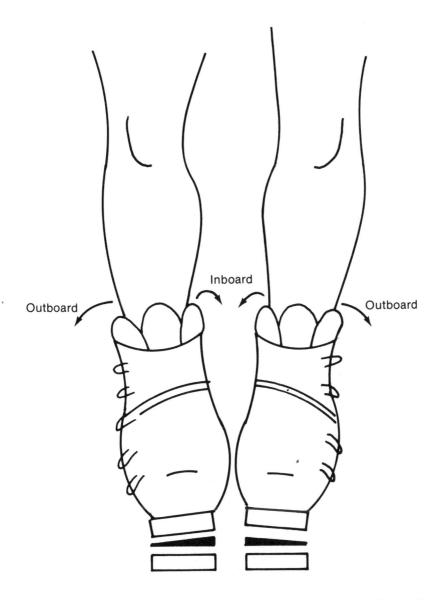

If you naturally stand on your outside edges, add cants or wedges with the thick edges *inboard*.

Racers are even more sensitive; some coaches say even young racers can feel half a degree of difference in cant.

Canting may be very important for people skiing in knee-high boots. Knee-high models give the skier so much leverage that minor motions of the knee are translated promptly into edging pressure. Likewise, minor variations in lower leg shape will turn up as relatively large changes in the orientation of the ski base to the snow.

Several conventional-height boots have adjustable cant devices built into the ankle hinge. These boots can be canted without installing wedges under the bindings, which in turn means you can still swap skis left for right. Obviously, if there are wedges under the bindings, swapping skis will have you canted in the wrong direction. Most Lange boots can be canted by drilling out the ankle rivets and resetting them in new positions. Ask a good ski shop mechanic for help with this.

One easy way to experiment with subtle canting changes is to pad the inner boot. A layer of foam padding inserted between the inner boot and the shell on the *inboard* (inseam) side of the boot cuff will place more weight on the inside edges of the skis. Padding on the outboard side will place more weight on the outside edges. A day of fooling around with sheets of foam can tell you whether you need canting and approximately how much.

If a canting test shows that you need less than a degree or two of cant, you can avoid installing wedges under the bindings by asking the shop to grind the boot soles. Or, if you have access to a joiner and you are good with tools, try it yourself. If you need more weight on the inside edges, grind some material from the outside edge of the boot sole; if you need more weight on the outside edges, grind material from the inside edge. Grind carefully and leave the boot sole flat all the way across. Be sure to grind an equivalent amount off the tops of the toe and heel flanges so the bindings will have parallel surfaces to work on. Also, have your bindings readjusted to fit the thinner flanges.

8

Boot Maintenance

Mildew can be a problem if boots are stored with wet liners. After each day of skiing, pull the inners out of your boots and let them dry overnight at room temperature. To keep inner boots from cracking, splitting, and deforming, keep them away from direct heat, which means away from the fireplace and baseboard heaters.

A boot-drying rack, with pegs on which to hang inner boots and a tray to hold the dripping from outer shells, is a handy item—making one can be a good project for a ski family. The rack can also be used to dry gloves, hats, and goggles. When my inner boots are very wet I bend a coat hanger to hold them and hang them up where the air circulation is good.

Most flexible plastics have a memory. They tend to hold a shape once that shape is set. For this reason it is important to buckle boots before storing them, even overnight. Otherwise the shells may freeze in the unbuckled position and distort slightly when it comes time to buckle them up again.

Minimize boot sole wear by slipping on a pair of "Cat Tracks" or similar oversoles before taking off across the park-

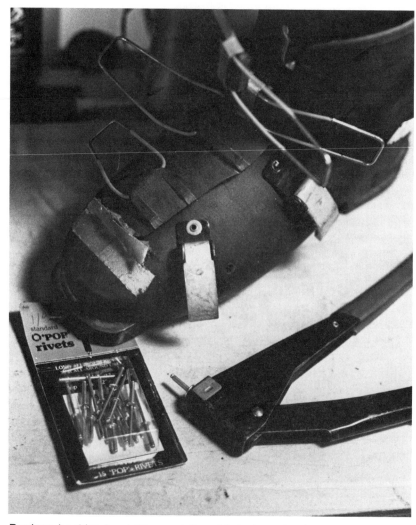

Replace buckles by drilling out the old rivets and using steel pop rivets and backup washers to install new buckles. Note that the toe dam on this beat-up old boot has been resealed with silicone sealer and duct tape.

ing lot. Always clean dried mud off boots before storing them or before stepping into bindings.

After a long period of storage you may find that your boot fit has changed. Boots that contain pockets of flow material are usually the culprits: the flow settles to the bottom of the pocket over a period of time. Gently warm the inside of the boot with a hair dryer to soften the flow material and knead it to redistribute it throughout the ankle and instep area.

Keep boots warm in transport. If they have to travel in the trunk of your car Friday night, bring them indoors to warm up before trying to get into them Saturday morning.

You can avoid most buckle damage by making sure the lower buckles are always closed. An open buckle lever is easy to snap off. Some buckles are placed in such a way that heavy powder snow tends to lift them open. You can grind the ends of the buckles so they will lie flat against the boot shell or make a flap of duct tape in front of the buckle to keep snow from getting underneath it.

9

Repairing Boots

Boots wear out. It's as simple as that. I ski about 60 days a year, and it's not uncommon to see a pair of brand-new boots go to hell in that period of time. Inner boot padding beds down so the boots seem to grow too large; tongues split or deform; soles, especially at the heel, wear out from walking, so they no longer fit the bindings; buckles bend or break off; buckle cables fray and break; shells split. I know a patrolman who broke seven pairs of Scotts in a single season and kept the last pair going with strapping tape and epoxy resin, after Scott told him he would henceforth be excluded from their warranty program. The following year he skied in Langes. It took him two seasons to break those.

Solve inner boot wear the same way you would treat a fitting problem: by taping foam sheet to the outside of the inner boot to restore the boot's original fit. This is tough to do when the boot was originally lined with fleece or fake fur, because as the material wears down to the base fabric you can easily lose a full size—one excellent reason not to buy boots so lined. Split liners can be taped over or delivered to your local shoe repairman for a neat stitch-up. Be sure that the fit of the inner boot won't be affected by any stitched repairs.

Many good-quality boots now incorporate a replaceable rubber heel, so when it wears out you can simply install a new one. A shop equipped with a hot-air welder can also restore the original contours of a plastic-heeled boot. Another way to restore the heel is to grind out a section of plastic around the worn area, without grinding all the way through the shell, and screw in a sheet of polyurethane or polyethylene cut to fit. Then grind the new section to shape. Seal the edges of the patch with silicone cement or epoxy. One good source of polyurethane sheet for this purpose is the flexible sleds sold in toy stores; they come rolled up. Just flatten the sled out and cut. After any heel restoration, the binding should be rechecked and readjusted by someone who knows how to do it.

Split shells can be repaired only by welding the plastic with a hot-air welder. These machines sell for more than $350, so you'll find them only in well-equipped ski shops. Minor leaks— at the toe dam or around the bottom of the cuff, for instance— can be sealed with silicone sealer or duct tape. If you ski in a lot of powder in a favorite pair of old boots, you may find it necessary to reseal the toe dam every year.

Broken buckles are fairly easy to replace. Drill out the old rivets and install a new buckle with pop rivets or tee nuts. Any good ski shop can sell replacement buckles and should be able to install a good-as-new rivet for a dollar or so.

PART III
BINDINGS

10

Binding Maintenance

In order to function properly, bindings must be clean, free of corrosion, and properly lubricated. Fortunately, it's easy to keep them in that condition.

Road grime and salt are the binding's worst enemies. It is vital to protect bindings from road spray either by bagging your skis, using one of the zippered binding sleeves supplied by the binding manufacturers, or simply by wrapping them in plastic bags secured by rubber bands. If bindings do ride cartop unprotected, rinse them with clean water before storing your skis—and rinse skis' steel edges at the same time.

Use an old toothbrush to clean mud out of binding toe and heel cups and from around all hinges and pivots. Dry the clean binding and lubricate it with a healthy dose of silicone spray.

It's always a good idea to inspect your bindings before filing and waxing skis. Obviously, before starting work on the ski edges you have to remove or lock up the ski brake. While you are looking at the binding, check the following points.

Antifriction Pad

Is it clean and smooth? Bits of gravel stuck in the boot sole can score the antifriction pad or even gouge sections out. I've seen the soft Teflon section of antifriction pads delaminate from the hard plastic base and spit off into the snow. Damaged antifriction pads must be replaced, which means a quick visit to a ski shop.

Antifriction Liners

Most modern bindings have plastic antifriction surfaces inside the toe and heel cups. Make sure these pads are clean, smooth, and solidly secured. They occasionally come adrift or fall out. If they are missing, replace them.

Lock up ski brake arms for base and edge maintenance. Use a commercial brake holder or a thick rubber band.

The window and trim have been knocked off this toe unit; to avoid filling the housing with snow and ice, replace the missing parts. Meanwhile, cover the holes with tape.

This antifriction pad is badly damaged and must be replaced.

Mounting Screws

All current bindings are mounted with Pozi-Drive screws, and trying to drive them with a big Phillips screwdriver will only ruin the screwdriver bit. However, you can use a number three Phillips to check the screws for looseness: if the screws turn at all, they are loose and should be tightened with a Pozi-Drive bit. Again, this means a visit to a ski shop.

If you do have a Pozi-Drive screwdriver, tighten loose screws carefully. Overtightening will strip the holes bored in the ski core or even delaminate a metal ski. The best bet is to remove the loose screw, clean it, place a few drops of white glue in the screw hole, and replace the screw firmly but gently.

Ski Brake Operation

Does the ski brake operate smoothly? Ski brake arms can often be bent. This happens more often in transport than in skiing mishaps—airlines are especially rough on things that stick out of ski bags. A bent or broken brake may not deploy fully when you need it or may actually prevent the boot from releasing from the binding. Repair or replace damaged brakes.

To check forward pressure adjustment, place the boot in the binding and see if the arrow in the heel unit lines up with the registration marks.

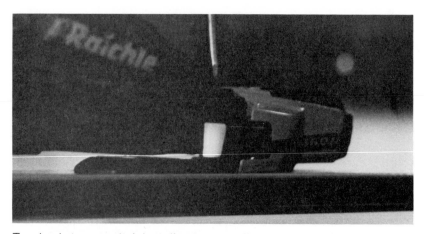

To check toe-cup height adjustment, pull back on the boot spoiler to raise the toe. Sight under the toe. One millimeter of daylight should be visible between the boot sole and antifriction pad.

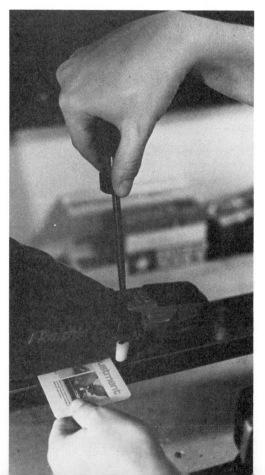

To adjust toe-cup height, turn the adjustment screw until slight pressure is felt on a card placed between the boot and the antifriction pad.

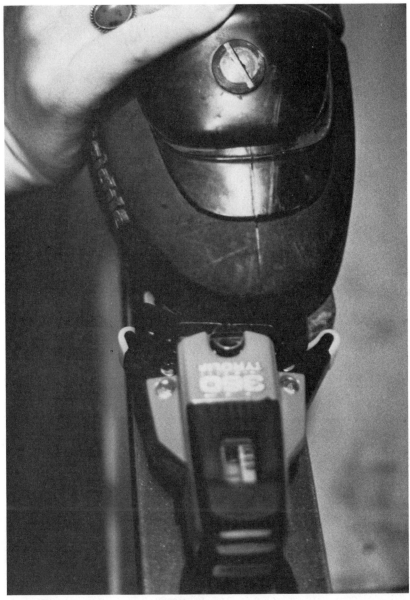

When binding is properly adjusted, cleaned, and lubricated, the boot will snap back to center when you've pushed the boot toe halfway out of the toe piece.

Some bindings (Geze and Marker, for instance) provide two toe-cup height adjustment screws. Adjust both.

Parts Missing

The clear plastic windows over the release adjustment scales and other trim parts can be knocked loose and lost while skiing or in transport. Cover holes in the binding housing with duct tape until you can find replacement parts. Otherwise, the binding can fill up with snow, locking the working parts. On some older bindings small adjustment screws can vibrate loose and be lost.

Pivot Posts

On single-pivot bindings the center post mounting can sometimes bend. This usually happens at the base, where the post is connected to the base plate. If the binding is misaligned, take it to a ski shop to be checked. If the pivot post is bent, the binding should be replaced under warranty.

11

Adjusting and Function-Testing

Binding mounting and adjustment are best left to properly trained mechanics equipped with the proper drilling jigs and tools. However, you should know enough about binding adjustment to know when your adjustments are wrong.

A well-known ski writer once phoned me for advice. All of a sudden, he said, he was having trouble turning left. His right ski seemed to have a mind of its own. He had filed and waxed his skis and checked to make sure there was nothing wrong with his boots. Neither ski seemed to be warped. "Well," I asked him, "is the toe cup on your right binding screwed down to the right clearance?" He called back 20 minutes later: "Son of a gun," he said. "That right toe cup was way out of adjustment."

First clean and lubricate the bindings and clean the boot soles. Inspect your boot soles carefully. Are there any unusual signs of wear? Look especially for scoring or gouges around the toe and heel flanges. If you find grooves worn anyplace where the boot normally touches the binding, inspect the binding parts for chips, gouges, or foreign matter.

Then place the boot in the binding and lock it in place slowly and smoothly. Make sure that the ski brake treadle isn't hanging up in the traction grooves of the boot sole and that the brake retracts fully. With the boot in the binding, pull backward on the boot's spoiler to lift the toe against the underside of the binding toe cup. Now sight under the sole of the boot over the antifriction pad. There should be about 1 mm clearance here. Check the clearance by sliding a playing card between the boot sole and the antifriction pad. If the card slides freely, tighten the toe-cup adjuster until you feel a moderate resistance when you pull at the card. If the card is clamped solidly in place, loosen the toe-cup adjuster screw. Salomon, Look, and Tyrolia toe pieces have just one toe-height adjusting screw; Geze and Marker toe units have two, one on each side. Make sure both screws are properly adjusted.

Now check the heel unit's forward thrust. Most heel units show an arrow, which lines up between two index marks when the boot is in place. If the arrow doesn't line up with those marks, take your skis and boots to a ski shop for a binding adjustment. Some heel units don't provide a forward-thrust adjustment index. These should be checked by a mechanic at least once a year.

Many heel units are self-adjusting for heel-cup height. Some, however, do have a heel-cup height adjuster. If your ski brake won't retract fully, see if the heel cup is set too high. Lowering it may provide enough additional pressure to retract the brake fully. If you crank in too much heel cup downthrust, however, it will clamp the heel and reduce the binding's efficiency in twist-out release.

After your bindings have been adjusted for release tension by a good mechanic, make a permanent note of the settings for both heels and toes. Each time you check the bindings, be sure the release value on the index scales hasn't changed. If it has, reset it to the original value.

As bindings get older, metal fatigue makes the release springs softer, and it becomes easier to twist out. On many bindings tired springs can be replaced; check this with your mechanic.

Now push the boot toe sideways against the resistance of the toe piece. Do this by hand or by knocking the toe of the boot sideways with a hammer. The boot should move out at least half an inch to either side and still snap back smoothly to center, or very close to center. If it won't move out or won't move back, it's time for a professional inspection.

Finally, if everything looks right and works smoothly, do a binding release self-test. The self-test should be performed every morning before you get on the lift. Just stand there in your boots and skis, edge one ski against the hardpack at the base area, and drive the boot toe sideways out of the binding. You should be able to do this under muscle power alone, to the right and to the left out of both bindings. If you can't, the bindings may be set too tight, or there may be some mechanical obstruction between the boot and binding or between the boot and ski. Clean your boot soles and try again.

PART IV
POLES AND GOGGLES

12

Pole Repair

Poles are simple, and pole repair is simple. Aluminum poles either bend or break. The straps wear out or break. The baskets break or slip off.

Pole shafts come in several grades. At the top of the heap are the hard, springy, lightweight shafts made of 7,000-series aluminum alloy. This alloy is high in additives—mostly magnesium and zinc—which make it very strong and stiff, but which also make it brittle. The 7,000-series alloys are very difficult to bend, and when they do deform too far they fracture with a clean, sharp break. A broken pole can't be repaired.

Most poles are of a slightly softer 6,000-series alloy, with fewer additives and a lower bending strength. The 6,000-series alloys will bend under impact—as when you fall on your pole.

A moderate bend can be repaired. Wrap the pole with duct tape just below the bend and lock it in a heavy vise. Wearing gloves and safety glasses, grasp the end of the pole firmly and bend it back straight. Be careful and watch carefully for any signs of breaking. The metal is permanently weakened at the bend site and you can expect it to bend there again. Eventually

it will break after repeated repairs. If you need more leverage
to bend a pole back straight, remove the grip and slip a length
of pipe over the end of the shaft.

The cheapest poles—those made of softer, nearly pure
aluminums—are very malleable. They bend easily and bend
back just as easily. If you're going to fall down a lot, stick with
a cheap pole.

Baskets are easy to replace. Cut the old basket off carefully
with a sharp knife. If necessary, use a pair of pliers or metal
shears to break and remove the old lock washer. Lubricate the
pole tip with some liquid soap and slide the new basket into
place. A new lock washer goes on last. It will slide on in only
one direction. Ram it home by placing the tip of the pole in a
hole bored through a two-by-four and smack the top of the
pole grip once or twice with a rubber mallet.

To replace a broken or worn-out strap, remove the Phillips
head screw from the top of the grip. Sometimes this screw is
covered by a small plastic plug. Dig it out with a small
screwdriver. Once the screw has been removed, the pole strap
just pulls out. Stick the new one in, line up the brass grommet
with the hole in the grip, and replace the screw and its plastic
cap.

Some more recent pole designs use a snap-in anchor for the
strap. These are usually quite simple to remove and replace.

If you want to replace the grip with a more comfortable
platform or strapless grip, remove the screw if there is one,
then just twist the old grip off the shaft. Make sure the new
grips will fit your shaft. Most American-made poles use a ¾-
inch outside-diameter shaft, while most European poles are
slightly smaller, with an 18 mm shaft. Push the new grip on as
far as it will go and tap it home with a mallet. Replace the
screw if a hole has been provided for it.

To shorten a pole, remove the grip. Measure off the amount
to be removed and score the aluminum shaft at this point with
the edge of a file. Hacksaw through the shaft and use the file to
smooth off the remaining sharp aluminum edges. If the top of
the shaft contained a wooden plug, use a drift to drive the plug

out and reinstall it in the top of the shortened shaft. These plugs are usually held in place by a dimple driven into the side of the shaft. Drive a new dimple into the top of the shortened shaft, using a center-punch or a large nail. Install the grip.

What usually breaks high-quality poles is nicks caused by the steel edges of your skis. You can protect a pole from edge damage by wrapping a layer of duct tape around its lower end. Unfortunately, this makes the pole considerably heavier.

The steel tips of poles are occasionally knocked loose and lost. Some ski shops sell replacement tips, which can be epoxied in place.

13

Goggles

The most common problem with goggles is scratched and cracked lenses. If your goggle lenses are damaged beyond repair, and you can no longer find replacements, the solution is simple. Drop in at your friendly local motorcycle dealership and see if it stocks the lens you need. If not, buy a polycarbonate motorcycle face shield. Using your old, damaged lens as a pattern, cut out a replacement lens. Polycarbonate is tough stuff; you'll need a very sharp knife or a pair of small metal shears for the job.

Lenses continually popping out or peeling loose? Glue them in place with an automotive silicone sealer. It makes a good, flexible, waterproof bond, and you can peel it away when it comes time to replace the lens.

Goggle straps can be repaired or replaced by anyone who knows how to use a sewing machine. Use a zigzag stitch, if possible, to keep the elastic stretchy. Goggles worn over a racing helmet need extralong straps. Most competition goggles are sold with long straps, but a favorite pair of recreational goggles can be converted to helmet use by sewing in an extra length of elastic material. Check first to make sure the goggle frames will fit under the helmet's face opening.

Use silicone sealer to glue back the foam that seals off the goggle frame vents when it starts to come adrift. If you want to use a favorite pair of inexpensive open-vent goggles for deep powder skiing, find some thin foam sheet you can cut to fit over the vents and glue it in place.

Many goggles can be customized to fit over eyeglasses simply by cutting notches in the frames under the straps to clear the temple pieces of your specs. Nothing yet discovered by man will keep your glasses from fogging inside the goggles. Your only alternative is the superexpensive electric fan goggles. The liquid antifog solutions work for a while and then evaporate or dissolve the first time you conduct a face-plant test.

Appendix A: Glossary

Antifriction pad—A Teflon pad attached to the ski, usually via the toe unit of the binding, on which the toe of the boot rests. It is designed to reduce friction between the boot sole and the ski top, especially during forward-weighted twisting falls, historically the most dangerous kind of falls.

Base wax—A sealer wax, used for impregnating new ski bases and as a base for racing waxes.

Chatter—Instability of the ski, often caused by excessive vibration; usually most noticeable on very hard snow.

Concave—A ski base is said to be concave when the polyethylene base is dished lower than the hard steel edges. *Railing* is a similar condition.

Convex—A ski is said to be convex when the edges are worn down below the level of the polyethylene base.

Cracked edge—A type of one-piece steel edge with very narrow gaps machined partway through it. The purpose of the cracks is to minimize the influence of the springy steel edge on the ski's dynamic and flex characteristics. To compensate for the loss of edge stiffness, skis with cracked edges are normally thicker, which makes them both torsionally stiffer and damper (see *damping*). These are desirable characteristics for slalom racing skis, and many first-rate slalom skis have cracked edges.

Continuous edge—A one-piece steel edge with a smooth, uninterrupted contact length. The continuous steel edge is the strongest part of any ski. A continuous edge glides more quickly than a cracked edge, so giant slalom and downhill skis are built with continuous edges. Handmade racing skis used by top racers generally have very thin, rather fragile edges, which flex easily to maintain good contact with the snow and which maximize contact of the fast waxed base with the snow. The nonporous steel edge itself won't hold wax.

Damping—A ski's internal resistance to continued vibration. Most of a ski's damping influence is derived from its contact with the snow. In softer snow, especially in wet snow, continued vibration is a real advantage, since it helps break up water droplets under the base and improves glide. On very hard snow, however, uncontrolled vibration can lead to chatter and loss of edge grip. Good damping materials are those with high internal molecular friction—friction that dissipates energy as heat, instead of storing the impact energy and then springing back. Steel and aluminum are lively, or undamped, materials. Fiberglass and rubber are quiet, or damping, materials. Damping is most important for slalom skis on icy race courses. Most of the rubber used in metal sandwich skis is only intended incidentally for vibration damping: its real purpose is to provide a durable and flexible bond between the steel edges and the aluminum structural layers.

Flex distribution—The pattern of stiffness along the length of the ski. Racing skis are generally stiffer than recreational skis, but there are also important differences in the balance of stiffness from shovel, to middle, to tail. For instance, most giant slalom skis are stiff in the middle and only moderately firm in the shovel and tail, while most slalom skis are moderately firm in the middle and fairly stiff at shovel and tail. A ski with forebody (section of ski before the boot) and afterbody (section of ski after the boot) that flex about equally is said to be

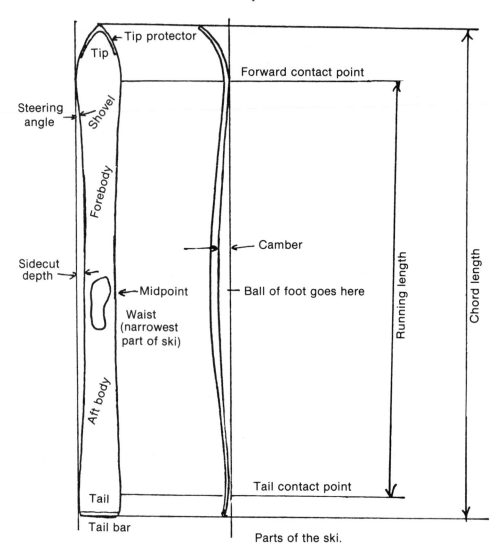

Parts of the ski.

balanced. When a ski has more than about 12 percent of its stiffness in the tail, it is said to be tail-stiff. Most skiers are better off in all conditions on a well-balanced ski.

Flow—In boots, flow is the generic term for the thixotropic puttylike materials used to provide an adaptable fit in some

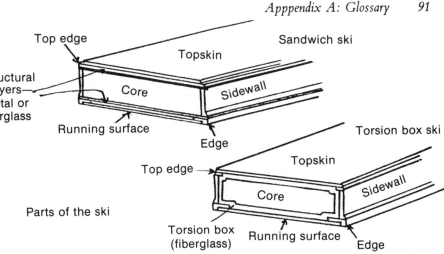

Parts of the ski

models. The flow softens under heat and pressure and conforms to the shape of the foot. It is normally contained in plastic bags sewn into the inner boot at critical fitting areas: over the instep (Hanson and some Lange boots) or around the ankle bones and sides of the feet (many Italian boots).

Hooky—Describes a ski that tends to continue turning while the skier is trying to get off the edge to start another turn.

Railing—When the ski's edges are raised above the level of the plastic running surface (see *concave*).

Release tension—The force that must be applied to a boot to release it from a binding. Release tension is adjustable, usually by turning a screw to preload a spring, which forces a bearing surface against a cam. Release tension can vary considerably since starting friction (the force required to get two contacting surfaces started sliding over one another) is higher than sliding friction. Thus, in a slow twisting fall, where forces build up gradually, starting friction may never be overcome, in which case the binding will not release and injury may result. Binding manufacturers are at great pains to reduce starting friction for this reason, and this is also the reason it is vitally important to keep antifriction surfaces on boots and bindings clean and lubricated. In a fast fall the impact on the binding is usually more than sufficient to overcome starting friction. Force equals mass times velocity squared, so if you fall at twice the speed, you exert four times as much force on your bindings. The corollary is that the slower you ski, the less dependable your bindings may be.

Sandwich—A type of ski construction in which upper and lower structural members, normally sheets of aluminum or fiberglass, are glued to a core of wood, foam, or some composite material.

Shovel—The forward part of a ski, through the widest and thinnest section and up into the tip.

Sidecut—Viewed from directly above or below, all modern alpine skis have concave sides—they are narrow in the middle and broader at tip and tail. The shape of a ski's side curve is referred to as its *sidecut* (sometimes as its *side camber*). *Extreme* sidecut refers to a ski markedly narrower at the middle than at the ends. All else being equal, such a ski will initiate turns more abruptly, and carve a tighter turn, than a ski with a straighter, more moderate sidecut, where the difference between the waist width and the width at tip and tail is less extreme. While the waist is the narrowest part of the ski, the tail is normally narrower than the shovel.

Sidewall—The vertical side of the ski, usually armored with a plastic filler to protect the core from moisture and consequent warping and splitting. This filler is usually a very hard, dense material—phenol or ABS. Some skis, however, use an elastic sidewall of rubbery urethane, and in many injection-molded skis the foam core forms its own sidewall.

Stability—A ski that is not oversensitive to small irregularities in the snow, and therefore feels smooth and solid underfoot, is said to be stable.

Torsion—The resistance of a ski to being twisted along its length. A ski that is torsionally very stiff drives its edges at the shovel and tail into the snow more aggressively and may therefore steer very quickly. A ski that is torsionally soft tends to follow uneven terrain better. Metal sandwich skis tend to be torsionally stiff, and so do skis with cracked edges. A designer must carefully balance torsional stiffness against flex distribution and sidecut to achieve the steering quickness and terrain absorption he wants.

Torsion box—A form of ski construction in which a spacer core is enclosed in a box of stiff load-carrying material, usually a plastic resin reinforced with fiberglass. The outer box works as a monocoque structure, and its dynamic characteristics are controlled by varying its relative height, width, and wall thickness. Most torsion-box skis are made by wrapping the core in uncured, resin-soaked sheets of fiberglass and are therefore referred to frequently as *wet-wrap* or *glass-wrap* skis.

Tracking—The ability of a ski to hold a straight course on every type of snow.

Waist—The narrowest part of the ski, in plane view (looking directly down at ski). In modern skis it is normally located near the heel of the boot.

Warp—A lateral twist or deformation in a ski. Warped skis can seldom be straightened permanently. New skis occasionally arrive slightly warped, and all skis should be checked periodically for warping. Warped skis should be replaced under warranty whenever possible.

Appendix B:
Troubleshooting Guide

Problem	Possible Cause	How to Fix It
Skis won't hold on hard snow	Edges dull or rusted or base convex	File for flatness, edge-file
	Skis too soft or too short	Test better skis
	Bindings don't grip boot sole adequately	Check boot sole wear, binding adjustment
Skis unpredictable in turn initiation, wash out at beginning or end of turn, skip or buck when edged at high speed	Edges dull at tip and/or tail	File for flatness and edge-file, leaving skis sharp to tip and tail
	Bindings don't grip boot sole adequately	Check boot sole wear, binding adjustment
Skis hook, won't come off edge, or won't swivel in softer snow	Edges burred or too sharp at tip and tail	Dull edges at tip and tail, round off tail bar and tip protector
	Skis concave or railed	File for flatness
Skis bog down or slow abruptly, unpredictably, when passing from hard to soft snow or sun to shade	Wrong wax or no wax	Consult waxing chart and rub on appropriate wax
Skis slow, sticky	Wrong wax or no wax	Apply appropriate wax
	Bases badly gouged	Patch bases and flat file

Problem	Possible Cause	How to Fix It
Skis "rudder," refuse to turn in deep snow	Skis concave or railed	Flat file
	Tails too stiff	Dull tails or use softer skis
	Skis too narrow	Use wider, softer skis
Skis turn better in one direction than the other	Skis warped or bent	Replace skis
	Edge of one ski badly burred	File for flatness, edge-file
	Binding loose on one ski	Check boot sole wear, binding adjustment
	Boots need canting	Install wedges with thick edge inboard
Skis unstable, wander apart; won't initiate turns quickly	Boots need canting	Install wedges with thick edges outboard
Skis continually cross tips even on smooth terrain	Skis concave or railed	Flat file
	Foot pronates inside shell	Add custom-molded orthotic insole
Skis feel heavy, long, awkward; won't turn easily	Boots too soft or too large	Test better boot
	Skis too long or too stiff	Dull tip and tail

Problem	Possible Cause	How to Fix It
Cold toes	Boots too tight over instep	Loosen instep buckle or remove insole
	Boots too tight around Achilles tendon	Remove foam padding from behind ankle pockets
	Boots stored wet overnight	Dry boot liners with hair dryer
	Boots leak	Seal toe dam with silicone sealer or tape; dry liner
Blisters	Boots too wide	Add padding to outside of inner boot
	Boots too long	Try smaller boot
Toes bruised under toenails; nail turns black	Boots too short	Buy longer boots or have shop enlarge boot toes
Muscle pain in thighs and lower back; mogul skiing too punishing	Boots too stiff	Soften boot flex
Unable to make proper forward-weighted turns; always sitting back	Inadequate forward lean	Add padding to back of inner boot, between inner boot and highback spoiler

Problem	Possible Cause	How to Fix It
Pressure points or painful hotspots	Flow material badly distributed	Warm inner boots with hair dryer and knead flow out smooth
	Boot too tight over painful spot	Remove foam padding from inner boot at site of hotspot
Pain or cramps over instep	Boot too tight over instep	Remove insole or grind footbed thinner
Pain or cramps in arch or vamp of foot	Built-in arch support too high	Remove insole and grind arch support thinner or replace insole with orthotic
Bruised shins	Tongue deformed	Steam tongue, re-form it
	Tongue broken	Replace tongue or buy new boot
	Tongue too soft	Reinforce back of tongue
	Shell too low and stiff	Reinforce back of tongue or soften shell flex
Shins rubbed raw	Tongue too sticky or abrasive	Tape plastic bag around tongue or spray with silicone

Problem	Possible Cause	How to Fix It
Bindings release too easily	Forward pressure incorrect at heel	Check and adjust forward pressure at heel
	Release value set too low	Check and adjust release setting
	Release springs fatigued	Return to shop for replacement
Bindings don't return to center after lateral test	Forward pressure incorrect at heel	Check and adjust
or	Toe cup height set too low	Check and adjust
Bindings won't release in twist-out self-test	Heel cup height set too low	Check and adjust
	Antifriction pad or toe-cup liners dirty, scored, or missing	Check condition and replace if necessary
	Dirt in sole of boot	Check and clean
	Binding unlubricated	Lubricate with silicone spray
	Too much snow packed under boot sole	Clean snow off boot sole and ski top
	Ice packed inside binding mechanism	Check and, if necessary, warm bindings to melt out ice

Problem	Possible Cause	How to Fix It
Boot won't enter binding or binding won't close	Too much snow packed under boot sole	Clean off snow
	Toe cup height or heel cup height incorrect	Check and adjust
	Forward pressure at heel incorrect	Check and adjust
	Heel cup treadle broken	Return to shop for replacement
Bindings loose, rattling	Toe or heel cup incorrect height	Check and adjust
	Mounting screws stripped or loose	Check and repair screw placement
	Toe- or heel-cup adjustment screws stripped or missing, or pivot post bent	Return to shop for replacement

Appendix C
General Guide
to Racing Wax Systems

Snow or Air Temperature		Toko System 4			Holmenkol Piste		Alpine Competition	
C°	F°	New, soft	Old, ice		New snow	Old snow	New snow	Old snow
+15	+59	Yellow	Yellow					
					Yellow	Yellow & Red		
+10	+50	Yellow & Red	Yellow & Red				Orange	Orange
					Yellow & Red	Yellow & Red		
+5	+41						Red & Orange	
						Red		Red & Orange
0 Freezing	+32	Red & Yellow	Red & Green	as snow becomes harder, add Violet hardener	Red & Yellow	Red & Blue	Red	Red & Orange
−5	+23				Red & Yellow	Red & Green	Red & Blue	Red
−10	+14	Red & Green	Red & Green		Red & Green	& Blue	Blue	Red & Blue
−15	+5				White & Green	Green & Red Green & White	Blue & Green	Blue Blue & Green
−20	−4						Green	Green
		Green	Green					
−25	−13							

Wet snow · *Dry snow* (left temperature column labels)

Fall Line		Slik	U.S. Ski Wax	Swix	Vola	Hot Sauce	Kwik
New snow	Old snow						
				Yellow paraffin (mix above freezing)	Orange		
Yellow & Red	Yellow		Paraffin & Red				
		Yellow					
		Yellow & Red		Red			
			Red				Red & Impregnation wax
		Red			Blue		
Red & Blue	Red		Red & Blue	Violet			Red
	Red & Blue	Red & Blue					Blue
Blue & Green			Blue				Green
	Blue		Blue & Green	Blue	Olive	Broad-spectrum wax	Green & Hardner
		Blue					
Green & Blue	Blue & Green		Green				
				Green			
Green	Green & Blue						
	Green			White paraffin (mix below freezing)			

(U.S. Ski Wax column note: or use Gold broad-spectrum wax)

Appendix D:
Where to Find It

The following companies manufacture or import ski maintenance equipment and supplies. If your local ski shop doesn't stock an item you need, one of these firms can tell you where to find it.

Alliston Ski Tools
2906 Pine Ave.
Niagara Falls, NY 14301
  Tools and supplies.

Alpine Crafts Company, Inc.
PO Box 2467
South San Francisco, CA 94080
  Vola ski wax, Supernaltene repair candles, files, scrapers, etc.

Basque Industries
4919 N. Broadway #20
Boulder, CO 80302
  Ski-tuning equipment.

Beconta Inc.
50 Executive Blvd.
Elmsford, NY 10523
  Fall Line ski wax, vises, repair equipment and supplies.

Cannedge Co.
815 Park Ave.
Minneapolis, MN 55404
  Boot-fitting aids, canting supplies.

Collins Ski Products, Inc.
Box 11
Bergenfield, NJ 07621
  Files and file holders.

Concepts Design Inc.
161 Main St.
Ridgefield Park, NJ 07660
  Vises.

Curley-Bates Co.
860 Stanton Rd.
Burlingame, CA 94010
  Toko ski wax and ski-tuning products, including vises, scrapers, repair equipment.

Daleboot USA
2150 S. 3rd West St.
Salt Lake City, UT 84115
  Boot-fitting aids.

Dicki Pete & Co.
Box 1053
Vail, CO 81657
  Files, scrapers, stones, true bars.

Geze Sports Products
208 Flynn Ave.
Burlington, VT 05401
  Holmenkol waxes, files, scrapers, etc., and Geze ski vises.

Gold Lode Inc.
1974 Ohio St.
Lisle, IL 60532
  Tuning equipment and supplies.

Hertel and Company Inc.
PO Box 10
Cupertino, CA 95015
  Hot Sauce ski wax, base repair equipment, hot waxing machines, ski vises.

Imports International Sales
1635 17th St.
Denver, CO 80202
  Files and scrapers.

K/F Precision Products
826 N. Winchester Blvd.
San Jose, CA 95128
   Boot-fitting aids, canting supplies, etc.

Kwik Ski Products
PO Box 98906
Seattle, WA 98188
   Files, scrapers, complete line of repair and tuning tools,
supplies, and wax.

Maxiglide Products Inc.
PO Box 302
State College, PA 16801
   Teflon-based waxless gliding formula.

Mohn Corporation
1345-D Silica Ave.
Sacramento, CA 95815
   Tuning equipment.

Mountain Tek
PO Box 843
Neptune, NJ 07756
   Vises, repair equipment.

Nafco Industries Inc.
PO Box 1893
Carson City, NV 89701
   Vises, tools, supplies.

Nordica USA
6 Thompson Drive
Essex Junction, VT 05452
   Boot-fitting aids.

Olin Ski Company, Inc.
475 Smith St.
Middletown, CT 06457
  Ski-tuning kits.

Raichle Molitor USA Inc.
Geneva Rd.
Brewster, NY 10509
  Boot-fitting aids.

Reliable Racing Supply
624 Glen St.
Glen Falls, NY 12801
  Complete line of performance tuning equipment and supplies.

Ski Accessories Co.
909 N. Milford Rd.
Highland, MI 48031
  Alpine Competition wax, complete line of repair and tuning tools.

Ski-Hi, Inc.
2928 Cliff Dr.
Newport Beach, CA 92663
  Files, scrapers.

Ski Kare Inc.
PO Box 716
Berthoud, CO 80513
  Vises, repair equipment.

Ski Tools Inc.
5428 Wilson Dr.
Mentor, OH 44060
  Tuning and repair equipment.

Sport-Obermeyer, Ltd.
92 Atlantic Ave.
Aspen, CO 81611
  Slik wax, tuning equipment.

Swix Sport USA
Tracy Rd.
Chelmsford, MA 01824
  Swix wax, tuning and repair equipment.

The Tool Company
Box 269
Bondville, VT 05340
  Tuning and repair equipment.

U.S. Ski Wax
PO Box 4386
Denver, CO 80204
  U.S. Ski Wax and tuning and repair equipment.

Wax Magic Ski Products
346-C E. Carson St.
Carson, CA 90745
  Hot wax machine, tuning gear.

Index